CAREER MAGIC

ENDORSEMENTS

Lee has a way of cutting through all the noise, bringing clarity, understanding, and vision to help us become our very best. When the smoke clears, clarity helps us to be laser-focused.

Ronnie W Farris, Director of Postal Services,
Lipscomb University

Lee walks the talk. His example and influence on how I view career moves and opportunities helped me become more pragmatic and purposeful about my own career choices and those of others. *Career Magic* is full of impactful wisdom and simple effective principles to guide your work life. Worth reading twice!

Corinne "Cruella" Winter-Rousset, CEO and
Founder of CWR Talent, London UK.

Career Magic changed my world. It taught me everybody matters, culture drives performance, and change starts with me. A must-read for all in leadership.

Dr. Charles Ireland, Duly Health and Care,
Division Chief of Urgent Care

I am thankful to have discovered Lee's content during college and while working at Walt Disney World. Lee's lessons in time management and customer service were influential while I was at a stage in my life where I was juggling school work a full-time job while also working to provide the best Guest experience that I could in my role. Now, years later, as a business owner, Lee has been an influential mentor in my life, providing me with exceptional lessons for elevating my career and becoming an intentional leader.

Cassie Tucker, Founder of CAMM Media

My personal and career opportunities have blossomed since listening to Lee's podcasts, reading his books, and joining the Cockerell Academy. Lee is transparent, concise, and a leadership model for me, my family, and many of my clients. Lee is a bridge between knowledge and action, resulting in increased confidence, efficiency, and empowerment.

Jeanne Williams, Career Consultant

Lee's advice has inspired me to live my personal values through my career without settling. If you want to do the same, I would highly recommend *Career Magic*.

Scott Anthony Barlow, CEO, and Author,
Happen To Your Career.

After reading *Career Magic* at a pivotal moment in my career, I was able to effectively plan for what was next. The results were two promotions and owning a successful business!

Tim Dyck, Owner, Best Culture Solutions, Inc.

Lee Cockerell has been a source of insight, guidance, and inspiration to me for much of my career. From leadership lessons in his first book *Creating Magic*, to time management insights in his Time Management Magic book and online course, to the stories and wisdom he shares in his Creating Disney Magic podcast, to the wealth of resources at Cockerell Academy, Lee has taken what he's learned from his decades of experience and shared it us so we can all take our careers to the next level. I'm a better leader because of the lessons I've learned from Lee.

Lou Prosperi, Senior Manager of Documentation and
Curriculum at Oracle Energy and Water, and author of
The Imagineering Toolbox series.

In 2008, Lee Cockerell launched my leadership journey with his first book, *Creating Magic*. His subsequent teachings, including *Career Magic*, have contributed to shaping and guiding my own development as I've incorporated his lessons learned into my own career. Lee has continued to serve as a powerful, and cherished, coach and mentor ever since, and for that I am profoundly grateful.

Jeff Dinard, Chief Information Officer, Vari

Lee's advice on tackling difficult situations right away has made a huge impact in how we address conflicts. We learned that open and immediate communication leads to positive outcomes. There are no obstacle we can't overcome when we work together towards the same goals!

Dr. Mariela Feldman, Ed.D., BCBA., QBA,
Executive Director, A Change in Trajectory

The Disney service model garners global recognition as being the "gold standard." The principles of leadership excellence, employee engagement, and exceptional service that Lee shares from his personal experience at Disney transcends corporate America and has universal application for all professions. As a law enforcement commander, I have applied these principles to strengthen service culture, promote transparency, and build community trust. Lee's down to Earth and common sense approach to applying these principles has helped me empower our team, as a whole, to personalize their "customer service," build collaborative partnerships with the community, and search for creative solutions to community concerns. Law enforcement is not commonly viewed as a "model customer service" profession – but it absolutely is and must be a way of doing business by an entire police organization, regardless of the role. When applied, the principles that Lee shares increases citizen motivation to report crimes, they build trust, increase officer safety, and fosters an understanding of expectations on "both sides" of the partnership.

Troy Fergueson, Law Enforcement Lieutenant, Florida

I was fortunate to learn about Lee early in my career. His advice has been invaluable to our team and me as we turned around a title I "D" rated school to an "A" rated school and became 1 of only 4 Kagan Model Schools. Lee's advice has helped me to have a magical career and will help you too. More importantly though, his advice will help you create an inclusive culture where others can have magical careers too. Thank you Lee for sharing your pixie dust with the world and helping us to create magic with our team, families, and students.

Evan Markowitz, Principal, Athenian Academy
Of Technology And The Arts

Lee Cockerell's tips and tricks for career and time management go beyond success in your career but apply to success in life. His words to always look for a better way and look for improvement help drive me professionally and personally.

Randy J. Rumpf, PhD, Supervisor, PreK-12 Fine Arts,
Montgomery County (MD) Public Schools

As an entrepreneur, it can quickly become overwhelming trying to navigate the onslaught of meaningful business advice while staying true to your purpose. However, any time I have reached out to Lee, whether it's for coffee or as an attendee at his Mastermind, he offers guidance that brings everything back into alignment through his practical, applicable and lighthearted leadership. Two profoundly simple statements Lee made to me over the years are, without a doubt, what helped me pivot from professional lows to living my purpose; "Find happiness" and "Don't justify. Just be."

Katie Currens, Speaker, Author, Business Owner,
One Spark Solutions

As a huge fan of Lee's books, *Career Magic* is fantastic. A down-to-earth read full of great information you can use. Not only does he write about leadership, but he was there for me when I started my consulting business! Congratulations, Lee, on *Career Magic*!

Jeff Conroy, Conroy Leadership Consulting

Lee's deep insights from a career spanning market leaders Hilton, Marriott, and Disney are delivered in an approachable, straightforward way that lets you immediately put them to practice. From time management to considering new career opportunities to building a brand around fantastic service and caring for the customer, Lee's advice has helped me distinguish myself in my company and industry.

Steve Athanas, Associate Chief Information Officer, UMass Lowell

I stumbled upon Lee Cockerell's podcast a few years ago, and nothing in my career has been the same since. I quickly found myself leading a team of people when I didn't really know what it meant to be a leader. Lee helped me work through those issues and got to the core of the problem: ME! I wasn't empathic, and I wasn't displaying trust with my team. Since implementing his advice, our team has been much more productive, and morale has increased. Many people claim to know the "secret" to success in business, customer service, and leadership, but Lee truly knows and, most importantly, shows how to be a great leader and have a stellar career.

Caleb Miller, Chief Experience Officer at Text In Church

Lee and his books have made me the leader I am, using his magic every day to make a difference. Lee's advice is ingrained in my habits and helps me say and do the right things as a leader, a mentor, a coach, a friend, and a wife.

Andrea Schwarz, Director Novartis Business Services, Novartis Pharmaceuticals

CAREER MAGIC

HOW TO STAY ON TRACK
TO ACHIEVE A STELLAR CAREER

LEE COCKERELL

FORMER EXECUTIVE VICE-PRESIDENT, OPERATIONS,
WALT DISNEY WORLD® RESORT

NEW YORK

LONDON • NASHVILLE • MELBOURNE • VANCOUVER

CAREER MAGIC

How to Stay on Track to Achieve a Stellar Career

© 2022 Lee Cockerell, Former Executive Vice-President Operations
Walt Disney World Resort

Published in New York, New York, by Morgan James Publishing in partnership with Magic Press. Morgan James is a trademark of Morgan James, LLC.
www.MorganJamesPublishing.com

Proudly distributed by Ingram Publisher Services.

Morgan James BOGO™

A **FREE** ebook edition is available for you
or a friend with the purchase of this print book.

CLEARLY SIGN YOUR NAME ABOVE

Instructions to claim your free ebook edition:
1. Visit MorganJamesBOGO.com
2. Sign your name CLEARLY in the space above
3. Complete the form and submit a photo
   of this entire page
4. You or your friend can download the ebook
   to your preferred device

ISBN 9781631958700 paperback
ISBN 9781631958724 ebook
ISBN 9781631958717 case laminate
Library of Congress Control Number:
2021953019

Cover and Interior Design by:
Chris Treccani
www.3dogcreative.net

Morgan James PUBLISHING Builds with... **Habitat for Humanity® Peninsula and Greater Williamsburg**

Morgan James is a proud partner of Habitat for Humanity Peninsula
and Greater Williamsburg. Partners in building since 2006.

Get involved today! Visit MorganJamesPublishing.com/giving-back

Career Magic *is dedicated to Priscilla. She put up with me for fifty-four years as we moved eleven times around the world looking for career magic. We finally found it right in front us when we realized the magic is family, health, and happiness. My best promotions were to husband, father and grandfather.*

CONTENTS

Acknowledgments

This was a fun book to write most of the time, except when I was reminded of some of the real downers in my career. I owe my success to a lot of people. If you find your name in this book, you were a positive influence on my career. I am sure I have neglected to mention some of you, but I have not forgotten you, and I will always appreciate you. Special thanks to my beautiful wife, Priscilla, for riding with me on the Big Roller Coaster of Life for fifty-four years.

FOREWORD

In the fall of 2010, I was getting ready to deploy to Iraq for the third time, then as a 4-star general and commander of United States Forces-Iraq (USF-I). The fifteen-month period was shaping up to be an incredibly challenging one. The 50,000 American troops who remained in Iraq would advise, train, assist, and equip the Iraqi Security Forces who were in the lead and providing for the security of their country. At the same time, our troops would still be facing a threat from a formidable albeit degraded adversary in Al-Qaeda. We also faced the very real possibility that the Iraqi government would not renew the US–Iraq Status of Forces Agreement, and we would be required to transition all military forces and equipment out of the country by the December 31, 2011, deadline. (That is, in fact, what happened.)

The scale and strategic significance of the tasks that lay before us were tremendous. I needed my leaders, both officers and non-commissioned officers—most of whom had deployed multiple times in recent years—to be highly motivated, ready to lead, and able to think creatively. The success of the mission and the lives of our troops depended upon it. And so, as I have done many times over the years, I picked up the phone and called my good friend Lee Cockerell. I asked him if there was any chance he was available and willing to travel to Iraq to speak to the USF-I leadership. "You bet!" he told me. "Just say the word, and I'll be on the next plane to Baghdad."

Soon thereafter, Lee traveled to Iraq and spent a few days with our team at Camp Victory's Al Faw Palace. He sat and talked with young soldiers in the chow hall; he spent time with junior officers, lieutenants, captains, and majors, listening to them and learning more about the challenges they dealt with on a daily basis. He observed the close coordination that occurred between the military and members of our diplomatic corps, the embassy staff, and the thirty-plus-nation coalition. He spoke to leaders of all ranks—soldiers, sailors, airmen, marines, and civilians— and he shared with them his key leadership strategies and principles. Every person with whom Lee engaged walked away inspired, and his positive message resonated within the command for the remainder of what was ultimately a very successful deployment.

You may be asking yourself, "Why would a 4-star US Army general call up Lee Cockerell and ask him to travel to Baghdad, Iraq, to speak to a group of military leaders?" Here we had a former executive vice president of operations for Walt Disney World—"The Happiest Place on Earth!"— giving a leadership seminar in a combat zone! I promise you, as you read this book, the answer will become as obvious to you as it was to me. Lee and I are of like minds when it comes to leadership, and he has a tremendous gift for being able to convey in a very compelling way the principles that we both espouse. I have called upon Lee numerous times over the years and asked him to come and speak to my subordinate commanders and leaders. Every time, he graciously agreed to do so, and each presentation was even better than the previous.

I first met Lee back in 2000, when I attended a strategic leadership seminar for general officers hosted by the chief of staff of the army in Orlando, Florida. Then the executive vice president of operations for Walt Disney World, Lee was the final speaker on the program. By that point, we had listened to numerous presentations, and most of us were ready to call it a day. Then Lee started speaking; he spoke for almost two hours—without a single note or PowerPoint slide. Here was a guy who had spent thirty-plus years in the hospitality industry, teaching general officers about leadership. Yet, when he finished, every person in the room was sitting on the edge of his or her seat. It was "magical."

Lee spoke to us that day with the authority that comes from experience, and with the genuine humility that defines great leaders. He also demonstrated a real passion for leadership and a clear understanding of the importance of taking care of people. In his own words: "Management is doing things, getting things done, checking the box. Leadership is inspiring your people to accomplish the mission and taking care of them."

An army veteran himself, Lee often speaks about the traits shared by effective leaders in all professions, including the military and corporate America. They include a strong commitment to teamwork and hard work, a can-do attitude, humility, a passion for learning and pursuing new opportunities, and a willingness to help others succeed. Lee possesses an extraordinary ability to communicate his exceptional philosophy of leadership in a way that is easily embraced by others. However, it is important to note that the key to the tremendous success he has enjoyed is not the fact that he understands the leadership principles and techniques outlined in this book, but that *he lives by them.*

That night, after the seminar had concluded, I had an opportunity to visit one of the Disney theme parks. I made a point to stop in several of the shops, and I asked some of the cast members if they knew who Lee Cockerell was. I asked if they were familiar with his Great Leader Strategies, which have been used to train and develop thousands of managers at the Walt Disney World Resort. Every person I spoke with responded enthusiastically in the affirmative. They described Lee as a caring leader, present and engaged; they loved working for him. One cast member told me, "Mr. Cockerell isn't just a boss; he's an inspiring leader who takes the time to teach and develop the people who work for him." That was high praise, and very well deserved. I believe every leader should aspire to be viewed in such a way by the people they have the good fortune to lead.

In this book, Lee takes us on a personal journey that starts with his humble beginnings in Oklahoma. Through hard work, trial and error, and persistence, he became an enormously successful and highly respected senior leader at leading companies in the hospitality industry and eventually in The Walt Disney Company. He shares with his readers many of the lessons learned over the course of his extraordinary career so that they and others may benefit from those same lessons.

Once I began reading this book, I could not put it down. As a senior leader who has led troops in very challenging situations, both in peacetime and in combat, I can personally attest to the tremendous value of Lee's leadership philosophy. The genuine enthusiasm with which he conveys his message is both inspiring and infectious. I am confident that if you follow Lee's lessons, you too will create magic in your career!

Enjoy the journey!

General Lloyd J. Austin III
US Army (ret) and current secretary of defense

General Austin is a retired US Army general with nearly forty-one years of military service. He has the extraordinary distinction of having commanded troops in combat at the 1-, 2-, 3- and 4-star levels during his three deployments to Iraq and one to Afghanistan. Among his many notable achievements, General Austin helped spearhead the invasion into Iraq in March 2003 as the assistant division commander for maneuver for the 3rd Infantry Division. He later served as the commander of United States Forces-Iraq from September 2010 through the completion of Operation New Dawn in December 2011. He served as the 33rd vice chief of staff of the army before serving as the 12th commander of United States Central Command from 2013 to 2016.

In this capacity, he also served as the combined forces commander, overseeing the military campaign to defeat the terrorist group ISIL in Iraq and Syria. President Barack Obama, on the occasion of General Austin's retirement, said, "General Austin's character and competence exemplify what America demands of its military leaders." In 2021 General Austin became the secretary of defense of the United States of America.

INTRODUCTION

My career was magical—not because I spent so much of it at Disney, the company that creates magic, but because of the way I dealt with the many ups and downs that came my way. In fact, my career was magical because the journey was also sometimes tragical. It was like an exciting roller coaster ride, with calm periods when I was slowly climbing up the track and scary periods when I was careening straight down and around some very frightening twists and turns, fortunately with my wife, Priscilla, always by my side.

It will be the same with your career. Throughout life, it's not what happens to you but how you react to what happens that makes the difference. When I was the executive vice president of operations for the Walt Disney World Resort, I decided to write about my own career. I pondered how it had developed over time, all the lessons I'd learned, and how I'd dealt with each experience along the way, good and bad. In reviewing those decades, I realized that I've had just about every career experience you can imagine; from being a private in the US Army to getting my first job without having a college degree; from being fired to being passed over while pursuing my dream job; to finally receiving the most magical job in the world. And, after all that, I'm having more fun and success in retirement than should be legal.

I was moved to write about my career when I was still at Disney in order to help young people in the Disney College Program gain an understanding of the twists and turns careers can take. I wanted them to know they can not only survive during these transitions but thrive as well. Careers can go off the track at any time, whether you're twenty-two, forty-two, or sixty-two years old. My own ups were fantastic, and my downs were painful, and at times downright depressing. The important thing to remember during those sudden, steep falls on the roller coaster is that if you stay positive and understand that all obstacles in life are momentary, all you have to do is raise your arms, enjoy the ride, and climb aboard the next coaster, no matter how frightening it may seem. If you do that, I know you'll get back on track and be just fine.

I say that with confidence based on my own experience. I am now semiretired from corporate life, my career is better than ever, and I am having the ride of my life with my arms high in the air. The key to career development is recognizing what you learn along the way and making sure those lessons prepare you for the next step. No matter what position you hold, you have an opportunity to learn a lot if you pay attention, ask questions, and have a passion for your chosen career.

People are always asking me things like "How can I get ahead? How can I get into management? How can I get promoted? How can I make more money?" These are interesting questions. Here is what I think. I don't know exactly how you can accomplish those things, but I can tell you what I did, how things played out for me, and what I've learned. Remember, I'm taking a backward look to try to figure out what I did along the way that may have contributed to success in both my career and my personal life. I'm sharing advice with you based upon my own experience because that is all I know. Advice is just that: advice. So don't blame me if you follow my advice and things don't work out quite the way you'd hoped. Twenty-five years from now, don't say, "This is Lee's fault. I followed his advice, and it did not work out."

This is what worked for me, and I hope you will be able to take away a few lessons to help you when you make critical career decisions, both when things are going well and when they are not. Think of every obstacle in your life as a detour, not as a dead-end street.

I suggest you solicit several points of view on the subject of career development and then develop your own plan based on what you believe will work for you. Although you cannot plan for every situation that can possibly arise, you can anticipate things that just might happen as your career progresses and prepare responses in case they do. Reflection and anticipation are two very powerful methods for learning how you can do things better and which obstacles to look out for in the future.

The main purpose of this book is to help you achieve career success. But it's important to place that aim in the larger context of life. Success in the business world is only one measurement of true success. People with great career success, as measured by the position they've achieved and the money they've made, have accomplished only a minute part of what true success is. I know many individuals with big jobs and big titles whose personal lives are a mess. Many are not healthy, and many are struggling with their marriages or their children. I do not consider them successful in any sense of the word. Having wealth and a fancy title is very different from having happiness.

What you do is not the same as who you are. The most important thing in life, and the real measure of success, is this: Are you happy and healthy, and are your loved ones happy? This is real success!

My recommendations in this book are the same ones I've given to my son, Daniel, and other people close to me over the years. Making difficult decisions and taking risks are part of the development process for careers—and for life in general. Everything from accepting a new role to relocating for work, from leaving a position to going back to school can be in the equation. Living without taking risks is a formula for disappointment. Don't be so careful that you end up with a lot of regret one day. Living on the edge is where the fun is!

First things first. When you think you're running out of time and you need to pick up the pace, keep in mind that most of us will work for forty-five to fifty years. Fast is not always best. Acquiring experiences is very important, but what's even more important is what you learn from each experience, and how you apply those lessons toward becoming excellent at what you do.

My guideposts have been the three E's: education, experience, and exposure.

Education: Go to college if you can, but there are other ways to educate yourself as well: go to workshops, read, listen to podcasts, watch YouTube, try new things, travel, and ask Dr. Google anything you want to know. In the Internet age, if you don't know something and five minutes later you still don't know, it's your fault.

Experience: Get as much experience as you can. All experience is good, and while you're getting it try to be better than everyone else so you stand out.

Exposure: Get out of your village; go to the big city for five years and meet people from everywhere, every religion, every color, every education level, every language, every culture every sexual orientation. This will solve any bigotry and racism that the place where you grew up and the people who were your role models may have embedded in you.

These three E's will change your life for the better and open doors you never imagined.

Good luck!

Insights

Experience and exposure are the best long-term education.

Daily reflection and anticipation are powerful enablers.

Careers can and will hit obstacles.

Obstacles are detours, not dead ends.

Understand what real success is.

Make difficult decisions.

Avoid regrets.

Think every day about what you learned today.

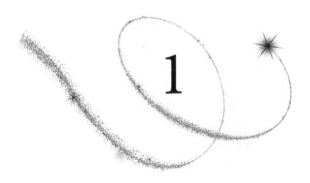

In the Beginning: 1964–1969

I'm going to tell you about a couple of early jobs I had—what I learned from them, and how they eventually helped me get to where I am today. This might be helpful if you are among those who think all the good jobs are gone.

The key is to make sure you're taking advantage of each experience in order to gain maximum knowledge, build a strong foundation, and forge solid relationships so you'll be successful in every role you take on. Excellence is always recognized because so many people do not operate with it. The real key is to always go above and beyond. If ten people do what you do, make sure you do it best by bringing to the job a can-do attitude, a passion for knowledge, impeccable reliability, and skilled performance.

I held twenty-two "real jobs" before I retired from Disney in 2006 to start my own company, and I must say I was the best performer in every one of those positions, in my humble opinion. I believe I was the best because I always went above and beyond, working harder than everyone else. My biggest fear was fear of failure, and I made my insecurity work in my favor.

I use the term "real jobs" because I define "real" as full time. These are the kinds of jobs that pay the rent and put food on the table. I had five part-time jobs before I had a real one, and I had my mom as a backup because I was living at home. Those part-time jobs do not count as much as the real ones—wherein if you don't perform, you don't eat.

I believe I achieved success in my career through a combination of:

- *taking risks,*

- *gaining a lot of varied experiences,*

- *having patience,*

- *being better and trying harder than everyone else at every job,*

- *being fully committed (meaning giving the job the time it needs every day, including six-day workweeks),*

- *growing in self-awareness,*

- *always learning from my mistakes,*

- *and most of all, having a very positive attitude, which I will explain next.*

Actually, I must add one other factor: I was fortunate to have two great mentors along the way who took a personal interest my development.

One of the key factors in my success, I believe, is the fact that I'm wired to be positive and to stay in a good mood even under stress. I'm also disciplined and well organized. I have a good sense of humor, and for the most part, I've loved all my jobs.

If you too are disciplined and organized and have a positive attitude, you too can make it. In fact, with those attributes, you can get by for a while without fully knowing what you're doing. Those traits give you the time and opportunity to learn. Everyone gives a break to people who have a positive attitude and try hard to give their best.

One vital truth about career development: if you do everything with excellence, your talents will stand out and be recognized. So, my advice? Be great!

- *Do great work, period! And don't be a whiner or make excuses when things don't go well.*

- *Stay positive no matter what, and do what needs to be done.*

- *Become an expert at whatever you're called upon to do.*

- *Make your boss look good.*

- *Don't create problems and extra work for your boss.*

- *Be organized and reliable. For help with that, see my book Time Management Magic: How to Get More Done Every Day and Move from Surviving to Thriving.*

Okay, that's the first bit of advice for creating career magic! Let's move on.

Humble Beginnings

I went to college for two years and made pretty bad grades. I never learned well in the classroom. I've always learned best by doing things, and then by teaching others what I learned. I guess if my parents had bought me Hooked on Phonics, Hooked on Math, and Hooked on Doing Your Homework or *How To Be A Great Student for Dummies*, I would have done better in school. But one rule I have is that you can't blame your parents for the mess you put yourself in. I was "Hooked on Fun," and "Hooked on Fun" does not prepare you for the real world, as I later found out.

I was born in Bartlesville, Oklahoma, and grew up on a dairy farm near Copan, Oklahoma. We were very poor.

Our house did not even have indoor plumbing. We had an outhouse for a toilet, and my mother heated water on the stove and bathed my brother, Jerry, and me in a big tub in the kitchen.

I attended what folks called a one-room schoolhouse in Antioch. It was actually two rooms in one small building: grades one through eight in one room with one teacher, and grades nine through twelve in the other room with a different teacher.

My mother was married five times. I was adopted by two of those husbands, and Cockerell was the third surname I had. I received it when I was sixteen years old. I would say that the odds of someone with that history becoming the head of Disney World operations were pretty near zero.

The lesson? *Never underestimate what you can achieve.*

My first job, at age eight, was to milk one of our Ayrshire dairy cows by hand every morning before going to school. We had electric milking machines, but I think my parents gave me that job for my personal development. Every morning I would put on a pair of white overalls over my school clothes (cows do not take days off) and then go milk my cow. I would sell the milk for 50 cents to our neighbors, the Thompsons, who lived across the road. Mr. and Mrs. Thompson had a peach orchard and gave me fresh peaches during the summer. That was my first lesson about perks. Fresh peaches were a nice perk for an eight-year-old and

50 cents was big money. On a side note, I have yet to find peaches that taste as good as the Thompsons'.

You may be thinking right now, *Why is Lee telling us all this? What does it have to do with career development?*

Here's why: *Your work matters at every level.* The discipline I learned when I was eight created the template for the work ethic I have carried with me ever since.

Unfortunately, many parents today do not give their children enough routine or hard work. Nor do they give them increasing responsibility as they mature, or hold them accountable for completing their tasks. I think learning good work habits early is vital. Make sure your children have lots of responsibility at home until they're old enough to get a job. Priscilla and I insisted that our son, Daniel, work in the summers, and he and his wife, Valerie, have done the same: their children, my grandkids, also work during the summer and have routine responsibilities at home.

While my grandfather drove the tractor, my brother, Jerry, and I sat on the back of his hay baler in the summers and made sure the bales of hay were tied properly. We thought it was fun. We cleaned up the barn after the cows had been milked. We did not think that was fun—except when we threw dried cow manure at each other. That was fun unless you were hit in the face. After fifth grade, we moved to Ardmore, Oklahoma, where my dad founded a trucking company to supply the thriving oil business. We were still poor, but things were a bit better, and we had indoor plumbing. By the way, my brother and I didn't know we were poor. We had shelter, food, clothing, and love.

My next part-time job was in a lumberyard when I was sixteen and in tenth grade. I was a minor, but that didn't seem to matter as much in those days. We unloaded train cars of cement, drywall, and lumber. The pay was a dollar an hour. The work was hard and hot, and it didn't take me long to know that was not what I wanted to do for the rest of my life. I became physically fit, though. Working on top of a boxcar in Oklahoma in August is an experience you will never forget.

My mother worked full time as a bookkeeper, so she taught my brother and me to do the household chores. We were expected to clean the house, do the dishes by hand, launder and iron our clothes, and do the yard work.

My mother did not mess around. She was very clear with us about what would happen if we didn't do our chores and do them well. Our punishment would include more than just a "time-out" or taking our cell phones away—obviously there were no cell phones then, and even if there had been, we would not have been able to afford one. We didn't get our first television until I was in the fifth grade, so we had plenty of time for household chores growing up. My mother had a great incentive program: when you finished your chores, you could play. That system always helped us focus and complete our work as quickly as possible.

Priscilla and I made sure our son had similar hard-work experiences. He worked on a cattle ranch in Oklahoma during the hot summers, clearing brush and digging fence post holes. Daniel made sure his son Jullian had a similar opportunity. Jullian worked in horticulture for two summers, pulling weeds and spreading hundreds of bags of mulch from 6:00 a.m. to 2:00 p.m. in 90-degree heat. He learned a lot about being on time, working with others, and following instructions. The horticulture company called it "The Stay in School Program." I believe it helped Jullian when he went off to college at seventeen and had to have the discipline to get up early and get to class on his own.

My mother wasn't moved if her kids were not happy every minute of every day; she focused on preparing us to be successful. Thanks to her, my brother became an orthopedic surgeon, and I ended up running Disney World operations. Do this for your children, and you will be giving them the best gift in the world: self-reliance! They will thank you one day.

My next job was in eleventh grade, delivering prescriptions for Parks' Drug Store. I wrecked the brand-new delivery car the day it was purchased because I was looking down at my paperwork instead of watching the road. The owner of the store, Henry Parks, didn't fire me. He told me to go home and take a nap. I will never forget how understanding and kind he was—and how scared I was. The lesson Mr. Parks taught me was: *Don't overreact to things*. If you overreact, you might do permanent harm to someone's self-confidence and self-esteem, especially a young person.

At that job I also worked the soda fountain and sold food, cigarettes, and other merchandise between deliveries. It was my first food, beverage, and retail experience. Because it was a real soda fountain, I could put as much or as little Coke syrup in a drink as the customer liked. Serving customers and learning to give them what they wanted was far different from cleaning up barn stalls and unloading lumber. In addition to the lessons I learned in that job, there was one great perk: air conditioning.

My next part-time job was in college. I was a kitchen steward in the SAE fraternity house at Oklahoma State University. I worked in the kitchen and dining room. I learned a lot about food preparation and serving, as well as how to be on time and work as part of a team. I remember I was serving dinner on October 22, 1962, when President Kennedy came on TV to tell us he was putting a naval blockade around Cuba and would use military force if necessary. That was the beginning of the Cuban Missile Crisis, which lasted thirteen days. I thought of JFK and that incident often throughout my career when I had tough decisions to make as a leader. My issues seemed like child's play compared to dealing with Nikita Khrushchev and the possibility of starting a nuclear war.

My next job, at nineteen, was working in the Oklahoma oil fields during the summer vacation after my freshman year at college. Living away from home, I rented a room in a boarding house. My job entailed helping repair natural gas pipelines and cleaning motors in a refinery. Sometimes the temperature reached 100 degrees. The men with whom

I worked were tough; they ate whole raw onions with their sandwiches at lunch while smoking cigarettes at the same time. They didn't care too much for young college kids, but by the end of the summer they liked me, I think. Maybe it was because I had started eating a raw onion with my lunch too. I learned to keep fairly quiet in that job, and to just do what I was told. I think those oilmen liked that and tolerated me because of it. That seemed to be the highest accolade achievable among them.

My final part-time job, after my second year at Oklahoma State, was working at Harvey's Wagon Wheel Hotel and Casino in Lake Tahoe, Nevada. I started that summer as a "grease man," earning $2.25 per hour. The job consisted of pushing a little cart around all of the kitchens and emptying the griddles of the grease that built up while the cooks grilled hamburgers, bacon, and other food. I can tell you that the job of grease man was not highly respected by the other employees, but that was their mistake. It's actually a very important job, and the experience taught me an important lesson: *Always remember that everyone in a complex operation is important.* Remembering that one thing will enhance your career dramatically.

Thinking back to my early days reminds me of managers I worked with who did not treat everyone respectfully. They looked down at people because of the positions they held or where they were from. Just the other day I asked someone, "Who do you think is more important, the person who orders the French fries, the person who immediately stores them properly in the freezer, the person who delivers them, the person who cooks and salts them, the person who serves them, the person who cleans them off the dining room table, or the person who sweeps them off the floor?" The correct answer is "All of the above." One of the most important things I learned during those early jobs was that everyone is important and you'd better respect them or you'll be doing those jobs by yourself when they all quit.

You do not last long without your team.

I earned $90 a week in that job and lost all of it every week playing blackjack in Harrah's Casino after work since there was really nothing else to do. There were lessons in that experience too, as you'll soon see.

My second job at Harvey's that summer was working the night shift in housekeeping. My job was to do turndown service, which included turning down the beds, tidying up the rooms, and cleaning the bathrooms.

One night while I was playing blackjack at Harrah's Casino, a security officer approached me and asked to see my ID to check my age. I showed him my fake driver's license. He asked me to sign my name the way it appeared on the ID. Of course I couldn't do that; I was promptly handcuffed and put in jail for four hours until my roommates could round up $100 to bail me out. In court the next morning, the judge fined me $25, giving me back $75. He told me and the other forty underage gamblers in the courtroom that he'd better not see us again that summer. My gambling days were over.

Going forward, my gambling consisted mainly of accepting career moves that sometimes had risky odds.

College Dropout Makes Good

I dropped out of college after two years and entered the US Army in 1964. (This is not the same advice I gave my son.) Serving in the military was pretty common in our family; three of my mother's husbands had been in the army in World War II. I was the first in my family to go to college. My brother was the first to finish, and as I mentioned earlier, he became a surgeon. For fun, I often tell people that if I had finished college, I would have had a really good job too. This annoys some college graduates, so I don't use that sort of humor too often, especially with Ivy League alumni, many of whom have worked for this dropout over the years. I also had a nice perk: no college loans to pay off.

When I got on the bus in Ardmore in September 1964 to report to Fort Polk in Leesville, Louisiana, for basic training, my mother was crying. She later told me she had almost died the day I was born and again the day I got on that bus. I was on my way to the scary real world, and she knew it! I didn't know it at the time, but I soon realized why she was crying: she knew the war in Vietnam was escalating.

I went to cook school in the army since I had majored in hotel and restaurant administration while still in college. I hadn't had much cooking experience before, but I could read the recipes and I knew how to follow instructions. If you think army food is bad, you don't know how much worse it would be if you didn't follow the recipes. In fact, army food is quite good. Don't believe everything you hear. There are different levels of good and bad.

I learned quickly on the job, and I must have learned well because I placed second in a class of several hundred cooks, just below a professional cook from England by the name of Terrence Biggs.

That experience taught me to have a great respect for following instructions. On one occasion I made dough for three hundred hamburger buns but didn't pay attention to when and how to add the yeast. I'll spare you the whole story, but I can tell you that I had a very bad day. I was lucky not to be court-martialed for ruining all those ingredients. My punishment was to do both dishwashing and potato peeling for the next few days, since the automatic potato-peeling machines were not working. I peeled those potatoes faster than anyone ever had, and I did it with a good attitude. As a result, I soon got my cook's job back. Another important lesson: *When you have a setback, stay positive, learn from your mistake, and work your way back up.* A mistake repeated is a decision. A bad attitude and poor performance will get you nothing but trouble and take you nowhere fast.

I also learned that if I was allowed to do something and someone showed me the right way to do it, I could accomplish just about anything. That was a good lesson in self-awareness, which may be one of the most important traits a leader can have.

I met two Brits in the army: Graham Cromack and Terrence Biggs, the professional cook who had beaten me out of placing first in cook's school. They were the first foreigners I'd ever met. In those days, anyone in the US on a green card had to serve in the military.

When I was discharged from the army, I went to Washington, D.C. with Terrence. Terrence had told me he was going to be the chef at the Washington Hilton, which was due to open in three weeks. He said he'd get me a job too. It sounded good to me. I was twenty years old, so what was there to lose? I thought I might as well take a risk. What's the worst thing that can happen to you at that age? There's a great lesson in that story: *Spend time with the number one performer if possible, so you can learn from them.* Knowing the right people does not hurt! In fact, having good relationships with others will be a major factor in your career success.

Going into the army was the third time I had ever set foot out of Oklahoma, and going to Washington, D.C., would be the fourth. The first time had been a day trip to Dallas, just ninety miles from my home in Ardmore, when I was nineteen, and the second was when I worked in Lake Tahoe.

We stopped in Ardmore, picked up my car, and drove across the country for two days, arriving in Washington, D.C., on March 1. We checked into the Twin Bridges Marriott Hotel in Virginia. Even then, Marriott hotels were ahead of their time. They had a drive-in check-in, so you didn't even have to get out of your car. The room was $8 a night.

Marriott only had about twelve hotels in 1964. In fact, I had never heard of them, so I thought it must be a little nothing hotel company. Boy, was I wrong! Today Marriott has over seven thousand hotels, and the company was destined to play a central role in my career. Never underestimate what you can achieve.

Terrence and I went over to the Washington Hilton the next day. It turned out that my buddy Terrence was actually going to be the room-service breakfast cook, not the chef. The lesson here? *Don't believe everything someone tells you.* Many people enhance their résumés, I have learned. I've also learned that all stories sound true in isolation, and there is always another side to it. I use that lesson almost every day. As they say, "trust but verify." I remember a guy who said on his job application that he'd worked for the government for two years. That turned out to be true. He had been in prison for those two years.

The Washington Hilton was in utter turmoil as it was just two weeks from its grand opening. The woman in the employment office said, "So what do you want to do? What job do you want?"

I looked at her with a blank stare. I had no idea what I wanted to do because I had never been in a hotel in my life, except for a couple of cheesy motels with ten rooms. I had never even been to a nice restaurant with linen napkins and more than one fork, one knife, and one spoon. So I was taken aback by her question, even though I should have anticipated it. In my house, you licked the food off the dinner fork and then used the same fork to eat your pie, and the only dishwashers back then were my brother and me.

I regained my composure, and through some quick thinking, told her I would like to be a room-service waiter. I had seen them on television movies and had noticed that they were tipped in cash. Since I did not have a credit card, cash seemed like a pretty good idea. Years later, during a stock market plunge, I learned another reason why people say, "Cash is king!" I wish I'd learned that lesson earlier, but I will always remember it. Experience causes you to think differently. Reading about stock market declines and experiencing them with your own money are two different things. Reading about other people losing their money is not very emotional. Losing your own money is *very* emotional, and strong emotions reinforce your memory.

The personnel manager said, "No, the room-service jobs are all filled already. You can be a banquet waiter." I agreed, even though I didn't quite know what banquet waiter meant. The only banquet I had ever been to was my high school prom dinner, and that was in the YWCA basement in Ardmore.

After being hired, I walked into the grand ballroom of the hotel and almost had a heart attack. It seated three thousand guests, they told me. I still have no idea why they gave me that job. The only relevant experience I'd had was as a kitchen steward in my college fraternity house serving twenty-five to forty people at a time. I guess a little experience is better than no experience at all. In fact, all experience is valuable, and you never know when a particular experience will pay off. I did list that fraternity food-serving experience on my application, as well as my food and beverage experience in the army. When you're young, many employers will turn you down because of lack of experience, so it's wise to get every bit of it you can.

The University of Hilton

I had no clue about being a professional waiter, but I was lucky. One of the banquet supervisors, Kurt, a German fellow, took me under his wing. Kurt told me to pay close attention; he would train me, and everything would be fine. I loved the man instantly. We all need to look for opportunities to help others. None of us had experience before we had experience, so give people a break whenever you can, especially if they have a can-do, positive attitude and passion. I call them high-potential people. The only thing they're missing is skill, and that can be acquired with training.

If it had not been for Kurt, I don't know where I would be today. His training really helped me become successful. If you're a leader, your job is to develop others. Be like Kurt.

First, I learned all the fancy napkin folds and how to skirt a table without clip-on skirting because it hadn't been invented yet. We skirted tables with tablecloths and without pins. We had to learn how to fold the cloths perfectly, so they would drop exactly half an inch from the floor. This is hard to do. I also learned where the glasses went and in what order, and into which glasses to pour the wines and the water.

Even today, I use what I learned in that job. Priscilla and I can have fifty people to our house for dinner and do it all by ourselves, without any help or a catering company. That position at the Hilton saved me plenty of money over the years.

From there, it was progressive training, observing, practicing, and most of all making mistakes and learning from them. I asked a lot of questions because I had never before seen most of the food we were serving. At least it was not prepared and displayed that way by my mom or the local restaurants back home in Oklahoma. I ate my first lamb, oysters, snails, and flaming cherries for the Baked Alaska ice-cream bombs, which I definitely never had in Oklahoma. Whoever heard of baking ice cream?

I was always cooperative. When one of my many bosses wanted someone to stay late or open early, my hand went up. That paid off later. All my bosses through the years liked that I did that. Some things never change. People want to work with those who are willing to go the extra mile and have a good work ethic and a good attitude.

I learned the job well and, if I do say so myself, became an excellent banquet server. I served Lyndon Johnson, president of the United States, at one dinner on the head table. I also served Senator Ted Kennedy breakfast while he was still in a wheelchair from a plane crash he had been in.

I served so many famous people that I can't even start to remember them all. Some were nice and gracious, and some were not. That too was a good lesson that would serve me well later in my career: *Be nice to people.* Don't get too big for your britches, as my mother would often say. I assure you that humility will serve you well. When you're a big deal, don't be!

I learned how to serve foods and beverages. I learned all about wines and how to serve them. I learned how to carve anything and everything. I learned how to open oysters. I learned Russian service, French service, and good old American plate service. I learned how to be a bartender. I learned how to carry on brief conversations with famous people and those who thought they were famous. I learned how to be professional in my personal appearance and to polish my shoes well at the risk of being sent home if I didn't. I learned to appreciate my fellow workers, who were from every country in the world. That taught me many lessons about the importance of diversity and inclusiveness, which I had not had the opportunity to learn while growing up in Oklahoma.

I learned how to work hard every hour, even during long and continual shifts that seemed to never end. Often, I was at work by 5:00 a.m. and was usually there until midnight. Then I'd be back again for breakfast the next day. I learned how to remain professional, friendly, and courteous even on those long, exhausting days. Lesson: *Stay fit.* High energy and stamina matter; they will help you be successful and help you deal with stress.

My experience at the Hilton also showed me the other side of what goes on behind the scenes: the theft of products by my fellow workers, their ways of deceiving the boss, and how to make the guests' checks larger so you get bigger tips.

I observed so-called leaders misbehaving and doing things that were against the policy of the company—or, at a minimum, against good judgment. Their mothers would not have been happy with their behavior. I did not have respect for many of them. I don't ever want to forget that lesson when I deal with people. As I say in my books and seminars: *Be careful what you say and do because everyone is always watching you and judging you.* Your reputation is at stake every second of every day. Value it and protect it. One mistake these days can find its way to the Internet and do permanent damage to your career. What goes on the Internet, stays on the Internet.

I experienced bosses and guests treating me as if I were nobody. I experienced bosses who never asked my opinion and who set a very poor example. I never once, ever, saw the general manager of the Washington Hilton. I don't think he was comfortable in behind-the-scenes areas. I worked with a lot of "managers" who did not understand the responsibility and meaning of leadership and being a good role model.

You might ask, "What are these experiences worth?" My answer is: you could not buy this course in a college. I know this because I had been to college, and these types of experiences were not to be had. The education you receive from experience does not go only into your head; it also goes into your heart—never to be forgotten. Things you learn wait there until you need them in the future. Experience helps your intuition and judgment considerably. Today's young people do not want theory. They want reality. College gives you theory. Experience gives you reality. Get both.

I know things that some people will never know. I was able to see things in that serving job that some people will never see. I saw and did things at the young age of twenty that helped me become a better manager and leader. The experience helped me know when I was doing things right and when I was doing things wrong.

Another positive side of the job was that I made a lot of money. It was 1965, and I earned $13,000 in nine months. That enabled me to take the summer off to go to the beach in Atlantic City. The downside was that I worked day and night. In those days, our schedule was posted only three days in advance, so it was difficult to plan for travel or recreation. That too is a lesson: *Every job has good things and things that are not so good.* Such is life. There are good days and bad days.

I learned about unions and was a member of the Hotel Employees and Restaurant Employees Union (HERE). Eventually, I'd be on both sides of the labor-management divide, and I came to understand both positions clearly. It definitely helped a great deal later on in my career, when I was involved in union negotiations as an executive at Disney. Do not underestimate the importance of understanding the people on the other side, or the importance of the art of compromise.

I was able to take summers off because that's not a busy time for large convention hotels. The summer I spent in Atlantic City was long before any casinos were there. It was just a nice resort town. I loved the boardwalk and the beach. As soon as I arrived there, I found a room at the Kentucky Hotel for $10 a week. The place was scary and would have surely burned down in sixty seconds if there had been a fire. Next, I started looking for a job. I found one rather quickly at Luigi's Italian restaurant on Pacific Avenue. I got the job because of my experience as a waiter at the Washington Hilton. As I said before, all experience has value.

It was one of the best summers of my life. I worked five days a week from 4:00 to 9:00 p.m. and had fun the other nineteen hours of the day. I will keep those stories to myself. I made between $25 and $30 in cash tips every night. Back in those days, hardly anyone paid with a credit card.

Again, I learned a lot. Being a banquet server is different from being a restaurant server. Among other things, I learned all about Italian food. The owner provided meals to employees, but the only meal we could have was spaghetti and tomato sauce with Italian bread. We couldn't even have meat sauce or meatballs. So I had the same meal every day for three months. After a few weeks, I moved in with twenty other young people in a big house on Atlantic Avenue. We paid $10 per week each. The house was great. There was a twenty-four-hour poker game in the kitchen the whole summer. I did not participate, remembering my gambling problem in Lake Tahoe the summer before.

I think every young person should try to get a server's job. It teaches one to be organized and composed while quickly thinking on one's feet and at the same time serving all kinds of people. Some leave big tips, and some leave nothing. When our son, Daniel, was old enough, we made sure he had a server's job at Phillips Crab House in Ocean City, Maryland, and during college at the Copley Marriott in Boston. When our grandsons, Jullian and Tristan, were old enough, they worked at the French Pavilion at Epcot, and our granddaughter, Margot, worked in food service at the Magic Kingdom. Serving is one of the best jobs in the world for introverts. A person starts as an introvert in June and by the end of the summer is an extrovert.

When the summer ended in September, I headed back to the Washington Hilton and my full-time job serving banquets. After a few months, however, I decided that I wanted to get an office job so I could have more consistency in my schedule, take weekends off, and go home at 5:00 p.m. I heard that a position was available in the food and beverage accounting department, but it was a clerical job. I applied and was turned down because I did not have any experience in that line of work. I told the manager of the department that I had taken accounting twice in college, but that didn't impress him one bit.

About two months later, the food control manager came looking for me and asked if I still wanted the job. I said yes. I thought that I had just gotten my big break, but it turned out he offered me the job because he could not find anyone else to take it. Why? Because the salary was $80 a week. At the time, I was making several times that much as a banquet server.

Since I was single, I figured I would find a way to make the low salary work. My apartment, just down the street from the Hilton, was $52 a month, and I got most of my meals free at the hotel. If you want experience, you often have to pay the price. Don't worry about how much money you make when you're young. Instead, worry about how much you'll need to make when you're old. Do what you have to do when you're young so you can do what you *want* to do when you're old.

I accepted the food and beverage control position, but soon also had to get a night job as a waiter in a French restaurant in order to afford my apartment, car payments, and frequent trips to the discos and restaurants in Georgetown. My recreation expenses were high. I rarely ended my workday at 5:00 p.m., and the goal of time off on weekends never happened. I worked six nights a week as a waiter and Monday through Friday in the clerk's job. I did get Sundays off, so that was an improvement. The upside? I learned how to be a server in an upscale restaurant, which was far different from being a banquet server. So I had another experience under my belt, and that would pay off later in my career when I became a restaurant manager.

I learned a lot during my time as the clerk at the food control job. My boss was "Mr. Organized." He taped a daily minute-by-minute schedule for me on the wall next to my desk, and I had to follow that schedule to the letter:

8:00–8:15: Go to chef's office and pick up food-transfer forms.

8:15–8:45: Price out transfer forms.

8:45–9:00: Go to food storeroom and collect food requisitions from the day before.

9:00–10:00: Price out food requisitions.

10:00–10:15: Take a break.

10:15–11:00: Price out beverage requisitions.

11:00–11:30: Audit each invoice for accuracy.

11:30–12:00: Do inventory of room-service bar.

12:00–1:00: Eat lunch. (Yes, lunch hours really existed in the old days.)

The whole day was like that, scheduled to the minute until 5:00 p.m.

My boss was tough, but that's where I learned how effective checklists could be. To this day I love checklists as much as I did when I first learned that early lesson.

Remember, electronic calculators were not even invented yet, let alone cell phones with task-list capability. We had huge manual calculator machines with paper tape that would do basic math, but they were slow.

My boss taught me a lot about accounting systems, how to analyze profit and loss (P&L) statements, and how to do unit P&Ls using a model for how to allocate indirect costs. He was French, and when we took the inventory of the wines at the end of each month, he would make me call out the names of the wines, which in those days were mainly French in big hotels and fancy restaurants. He made me call them out for two reasons. The first was that he wanted me to learn how to pronounce the names, and the second was that it made him laugh when this Oklahoma boy attempted to pronounce them. When he finally stopped laughing, he would take the time to tell me about the region each wine was from. He taught me a lot, and I'm grateful for his instruction; when I lived in France twenty-three years later, I could pronounce the names of the wines when I went out to dinner. My French is still poor, but I can pronounce French wines properly.

I gained a lot in that position. The experiences were wonderful. Looking back, I realize that I had not earned a lot, but I truly learned a lot. As you can see, if you remove the L from *learned*, you have the word *earned*, and that's how you should think about experiences. What you walk away with is yours to keep forever, and to use both for your own benefit and as a gift to others. When you have done the job yourself, your credibility as a leader increases dramatically among those doing the same job.

You should learn new things every day in every position you hold. This is a surefire way to both stay interested and prepare for the next opportunity.

I often heard the cast members in the Disney College Program say that they couldn't learn anything in the jobs we assigned them. I know that this is not true. If you pay attention, you can learn a great deal in any job. You only need the desire to learn and the willingness to ask questions. These days, you have no excuse for not learning; you have Google at your fingertips.

Just remember that every experience in life can be a good experience in one way or another if you choose to see it that way. The things I learned from my early jobs were extremely valuable and continue to serve me well today. My pay may have been low, but I earned a million dollars' worth of experience.

Next, I'll review the two jobs I had after I became the best food control clerk I could be, and I will show you how I earned my next million in experience!

Insights

Excellence is a state of mind.

Make sure you *are* the best (attitude, passion, skill).

Take calculated risks.

Be great in everything you do.

Be organized and reliable, and keep your word.

All experience has value. Learning is your responsibility.

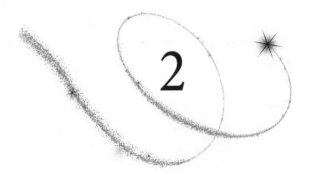

2

Marriage, Baby, Management, and the Big Apple: 1968–1969

Now, the question was: What do I do with the million dollars of experience I've earned? I decided I would try to leverage that million into several million more by investing it in more experience and more exposure.

As one of my bosses told me way back when, "Lee, worry about the position you have and not the one you want." He was saying that if you do a great job in the role you have, you will never have to worry about the next job or your dream job. He also meant that you should stay focused and be the best that you can be in every way, including attitude, professional appearance, work ethic, quality of work, timeliness, communication, continuous learning, and so on. Do this, and the next job will arrive just around the time you're ready for it. When you do a great job, it does not take long before someone notices, because so many others are doing only enough to get by. *Be better than everybody else.*

Remember, the purpose of this book is to give you food for thought. If you can begin to think differently, you can start acting and performing differently. With self-awareness, drive, continuous learning, commitment, and a little patience, I know that what Walt Disney himself once said is true: "If you can dream it, you can do it." If you want to be more and do more, you need to know more. That is what education, experience, and exposure provide you.

I continue to make this point: in every single experience you have, you can learn something that you can use in the future. *Begin to think about every experience as an opportunity to learn.*

I am not telling you that I felt this way when I was in some of my early positions. I, like many people, did not understand the value of experience and exposure, and how they educate you in a special and lasting way. I know it now, though. You can learn from others who have been there. If I sound like your mom and dad, I'm sorry, but it's the truth. Parents teach these lessons and harp on them because they love their kids, and I'm doing it here because I want you to have a magical, exciting, and fulfilling career—and, hopefully, few if any regrets.

Looking back, some of my worst jobs, worst bosses, and worst circumstances turned out to be some of my most valuable experiences. Remember, I said "looking back." At the time, I didn't always feel I was getting good experience. I sometimes felt like I was getting the raw end of the deal and should never have taken that particular job. I felt underpaid, underappreciated, and overworked. Have you ever felt that way? If you say no, you're a very lucky person, so count your blessings.

Careers don't always go straight up. Like roller coasters, they go up and down, and after a while you learn that the scary downs are temporary as long as you stay positive. And, as you know, it takes longer to go up than to come down. With determination, you will keep going up even though from time to time you may have an upset stomach and wish the ride were over.

Sometimes these negative experiences are attributed to bad luck, a personality clash, being in the wrong place at the wrong time, unfair circumstances, and many other things. I can tell you that I had several ups and downs in my career, as you will learn in the next few chapters. Maybe hearing my story will help you avoid some of the same mistakes and hazards. When one of these negative situations happens, it's imperative that you pick yourself up and get going again. Ideally, you will have learned from each experience so the same thing does not continue happening over and over again. As I said earlier, a mistake repeated is a decision. You are not a product of your circumstances; you are a product of your decisions.

In the first chapter, I talked about my first three real, full-time jobs: as a cook in the US Army, as a banquet server, and as a clerk in the food and beverage control office of the Washington Hilton Hotel, a very large convention hotel in Washington, D.C. In fact, John Hinckley shot President

Reagan as he was exiting this hotel and walking to his limousine on March 30, 1981. What's really weird is that Hinckley was born in Ardmore, Oklahoma, where I grew up. My career turned out better than his.

Looking back, I realize that I learned more in those first three jobs than I ever imagined at the time I was doing them. I'll say it again: please remember that every experience counts.

Now, for my next two positions . . .

I had been the food and beverage control clerk for about eight months when the company decided to expand the role of food and beverage controller and to have someone of that position in every Hilton hotel around the world. Well, there I was when they started looking for management trainees to develop for the new role. I had the experience, and I had done a great job as a clerk, so I was selected for the management-training program. My decision to take a low-paying clerk job was paying off. Sometimes you just have to take a lower-level job to get your foot in the door so you can show how great you are.

I was sent to Chicago for a week's worth of classroom training to learn the technical aspects of the new role. The classes were held at the Palmer House, one of the most famous of the Hilton hotels. I came back to Washington, D.C., after the training and was assigned to the position of assistant food and beverage controller. I was not yet in charge of the department, but I had my foot in the door—and that was half the battle.

No one reported to me, but I didn't care. I had a business card with what I thought was a nice title, and it impressed some of the ladies at the nightclubs I frequented in Georgetown. Receiving a business card was one of the highlights of my career at that time. Do not underestimate the value of the little things for your employees.

In my new position I was classified as management. This entitled me to work many more hours than when I was the clerk, and I was unable to receive overtime pay. There were no exempt and nonexempt positions back in those days.

Because I was working day and night, I had to give up my job as a waiter in the French restaurant. Otherwise, I would not be able to continue in my new salaried role. Instead, I picked up work as a part-time banquet waiter. Even though I was a manager in the hotel, I was allowed to work serving banquet lunches at the Hilton during my lunch hour (yes, lunch was an hour in length—the good old days, I guess). I also worked as an on-call waiter on some of the evenings I was available. My nightly trips to the Georgetown discos were dramatically reduced. There is always a way to make money if you really want to.

Can you imagine that as a salaried employee I was allowed to work banquets as a waiter in the middle of my management workday for extra money? Those were the good old days, without all the government and company rules that say what you can and cannot do on duty and off duty. Between the government, HR departments, and legal departments, the good old days are long gone, and many people are poorer now because of the many rules and laws that limit their earnings.

Well, as you know, time moves on. It was not long before my boss resigned and went back to France. I was promoted to his job. Something always seems to happen if you prepare yourself and hang in there.

New Position, New Title

Now I had two people reporting to me, but I still had received only technical training. Not one person had ever mentioned management or leadership to me in the context of what is important! I was given a new business card that read "Food and Beverage Controller." I loved that card and promptly sent my mother and grandmother a whole stack of them to give out to their friends to prove I was making progress.

I did okay with the management part of my new job, which consisted mostly of administrative responsibilities and bookkeeping to keep food and beverage costs under control. Between making out more checklists for everyone and creating a good trace system, I looked like I knew what I was doing. I had never been trained in my responsibilities as a leader, so upon reflection, I believe I did quite well. I treated my staff with respect and was pretty flexible in meeting their personal needs for time off and that sort of thing. Today they probably would say I was a good leader, even though the leadership concept never crossed my mind. I grew up in Oklahoma, where neighbors help neighbors, and that's what I practiced at work. I recommend you do the same.

I learned a lot about being organized in that position because in a job that deals with numbers, things have to balance. I learned more about accounting in that job than I ever did in college. As I said before, I had taken an accounting course twice to finally achieve a D. In business, I made an A. Practical, hands-on experience is how I've always learned best. Don't write anyone off just because they don't have a certain level of formal education. Always remember, different people learn in different ways.

One of the first things I did in that job was to move my office next to Peter Kleiser's office in the main kitchen, because, well, "He was the man." Peter was the executive chef. He was the boss, and I wanted to be close to him—not only to do a good job but also to get to know him and for him to get to know me. He would end up having a big say in my future. Being close to the action is important. Don't isolate yourself in a remote location. If you do, you will be forgotten and become irrelevant.

My new office was right in the middle of the kitchen, with big windows overlooking the bustling action. The responsibilities of my new position involved implementing strong food and beverage control systems and procedures. Being located right in the kitchen, I was part of the scene. I got to know all the cooks, dishwashers, and other employees whom I was trying to control. Lesson: *Make sure people know you and see you often.* It helps a great deal in getting your work done, especially in an area like control and audit. And having comfortable relationships with people is vital for getting them to cooperate and help you do your job. In all my future jobs I made sure my office was in the middle of the action.

Chef Kleiser taught me a lot. He was an excellent manager. He had to have a team that could cook and serve banquets for three thousand guests and at the same time manage several restaurants. He was a great leader too. I observed how he led his team. He was a teacher, and he respected everyone at every level. He was tough but fair. He always ate his meals with his team, and everyone was welcome at his table no matter what position they held. I never heard him raise his voice or try to intimidate anyone as many chefs had the bad habit of doing in those days.

One time, I ordered the wrong melons for a banquet for three thousand people. I ordered Crenshaw melons when I was supposed to order honeydews. I'll never forget what Chef Kleiser said to me: "Lee, you can be a fool once or a fool all of your life. When you don't know something, ask questions—then you will know, and that way, you will only be a fool once."

The fact is you're really only a fool if you don't know something *and* you fail to ask questions. No one respects someone who thinks or even acts like they know everything. Being humble is a big deal; it earns you a lot of credibility.

So many leaders have not learned this, including me from time to time early in my career. It's usually a lack of self-confidence, along with pride issues, that cause us not to ask questions. I still do not do this as well as I wish I did. My boss at Disney, Al Weiss, asked more questions than anyone I've ever known; he was never afraid to say, "I don't understand that. Please explain it to me again because I don't get it." That, I guess, is why he was president of Disney World and later the entirety of Disney Parks and Resorts.

One of the other things I learned in the control position—and it's funny now, but wasn't then—concerns fifteen hundred avocados I ordered. I did not order them early enough, and one day before the banquet they were still too hard to use. I ended up spreading them all over the hotel's pool deck with blankets over them so they'd ripen in time for the banquet. To this day, I don't think I ever pick up an avocado without thinking about the importance of knowing what you're doing and the timetable you have to work with.

If those avocados had not ripened, I think the chef would have fired me for sure because, as I recall, the incident occurred not long after the melon mishap. Can you imagine being fired over avocados? That would be a story you would not want to tell anyone or give to a future employer as the reason you're no longer at your previous job.

I do know one thing for sure: the chef gave me lots of breaks while I was learning because I had a good attitude and was a hard worker. That alone might be the best lesson I learned. People can give you a break, or they can ignore you and let you fall flat on your face. A can-do attitude will often be your best attribute, even if you have to fake it sometimes.

While I was at Disney World, two college program students came to see me on the same day. The first student told me that the program was the worst experience of her life and a total waste of time. Afterward, she continued to let me know that she'd learned nothing while at the Walt Disney World Resort in the college program. The second student came to see me later that afternoon and told me it had been the best experience of her life and she wanted to come back after graduation. I predict that the first person will have a disappointing career. She actually told me that the job was beneath her; she thought that because she attended a highly regarded college, she should be treated differently. What she really needed was experience, and she could not see that. Her self-awareness was out of focus. Frankly, nobody cares where you went to school. What they care about is what you can do and how well you can do it. The three things that will make you successful are skill, a can-do attitude, and passion. She had only skill. Missing two out of three is not going to serve her well.

Both of those students worked in fast-food operations. The difference between them had to do with attitude and humility. I suspect their parents raised them quite differently. If I could interview a candidate's parents, I'd be able to pretty accurately predict what kind of employee their child will be.

I can tell you I'm as comfortable on quarry tile in a kitchen as I am on the carpet in public spaces. A lot of people are not comfortable backstage, behind the scenes, because they have never experienced it. As we say in food and beverage, the kitchen is the "heart of the house." The heart is a very important organ, is it not?

In the Windy City

It wasn't long before I was promoted to the two-thousand-room Conrad Hilton Hotel in Chicago (it's now called the Chicago Hilton) as a food and beverage controller. I learned a lot of different things in that new position. I had a larger staff, and the food and beverage locations were much larger, busier, and more complex.

We even operated commercial production kitchens and packaging for the shipment of food products to other hotels around the country. The legal and safety issues around this kind of operation are numerous, complicated, and tedious. We were shipping food across state lines, and it had to be prepared just right and inspected for all the correct handling and packaging procedures from start to finish, with numerous licensing requirements. There were many new things for me to learn and learn quickly.

The one big thing I learned in that position was that my authority—or what I thought was my authority—would not work without good relationship skills. I dove right into the job and started trying to change things. I started putting new control procedures in place without establishing the right relationship with the executive chef, who had been there since long before I was born. Our relationship became so stressed that he actually banned me from the kitchen and sent me back up to my office on the executive floor so I couldn't bother him anymore. In my previous job at the Washington Hilton, I had moved my office next to the chef so I could build a good relationship with him. I forgot to do this in Chicago and I paid dearly for it. I never made that mistake again.

I started over the following week by apologizing to him, but it took several more months to get to where I could start doing what I was sent there to do. That taught me this lesson: *You must touch the people before you touch the task.* I learned that you'd better take the time to build trusting relationships before you try to exercise your authority.

I also learned that I was not as big a deal as I thought I was. I knew what had to be done, but I hadn't learned that when you move to a new environment you have to start over because no one knows your capability. I was the new kid on the block, and some people didn't even want me there. Imagine that! I learned that when you get promoted, not everyone is happy for you. I always keep track of who does and who does not encourage or congratulate people on their promotions.

Your technical and management expertise means nothing if you can't get anything done, and when there's resistance from the staff, you can't get much done. You get things done with the help of others. This is where the leadership piece comes in. If I had known back then what I know now about the importance of great leadership, I would never have fallen into the trap of arrogance. Arrogance gets you nowhere; it's dangerous to both your career and those around you.

Another thing I learned was that it's important to meet in person with anyone you have a problem with rather than sending them notes or emails. That was part of the problem I had with the chef. I would send him memos and carbon copy his boss because I was too intimidated to go see him personally. I can tell you with certainty: this never works. I was pouring gasoline on the fire. Why had someone not taught me those things? Experience is a tough teacher. Making things worse, my boss was even more intimidated by the chef than I was. That put me in a very difficult spot since I couldn't depend on my boss to get me out of the mess I'd created.

One day my boss asked me, "Lee, how old are you?" I said I was twenty-three. "You can't talk to people the way you do at your age," he said. My age had nothing to do with it, actually, but he was right that I could not get things done by trying to intimidate people into doing what I wanted, which was what I'd been doing. That was a great lesson. It's probably a fact that the younger you are, the more finesse you need to have to be effective, especially with older, more experienced individuals.

I did get somewhat lucky, though, in that the chef retired shortly afterward and a new one replaced him. Things worked well from then on.

In chapter 3, I'll tell you more about how I salvaged my performance in Chicago. Meanwhile, let's move on.

On to the Big Apple

One day I received a call offering me the position of food and beverage controller in the most famous hotel in New York City—maybe the most famous hotel in the world.

The Waldorf Astoria, which is owned by Hilton, first stood where the Empire State Building is today. Then, in 1929, it opened on Park Avenue between 49th and 50th streets, where it would serve more heads of state than any other hotel in the world. It was a whole new world for the country boy from Oklahoma.

I had by then earned my second million in experience, even though I couldn't afford much beyond the basic necessities. I was now married, and Priscilla and I had just had a baby boy. Daniel had arrived on February 18, 1969, only a few months before Neil Armstrong and Buzz Aldrin landed on the moon. With a child and a new job offer, life was beginning to get very adventurous!

My move from Chicago to New York was a major promotion. My salary would increase from $8,000 to $12,000 a year, a full 50 percent bump. I was very happy because

I thought we were finally in the big money and we could live really well. I was thinking, *Wow, a 50 percent raise.* That was huge. It turned out that it seemed much bigger than it actually was because living in New York City was a lot more costly than Chicago. The lesson here is that if things sound too good to be true, they usually are.

Things have really changed since then. Back in 1969, Hilton did not give you an interview trip. You just said yes or no to the offer, and if you said yes, you moved. Hilton put you up in a hotel for a few weeks while you found an apartment at your new location, and that was that. I am not sure what happened to those who said no. I'm pretty sure management didn't want me to find out the cost of housing and other expenses in New York City before I said yes or no to their offer.

We did not have much furniture, so it was an easy and cheap for Hilton to move my family to New York. Once the three of us got there, reality set in very quickly. We started looking for an apartment. It was one of those bad days I told you about earlier. We finally found a place we could maybe afford. It was $350 a month compared to the $135 we'd been paying in Chicago. It was a small two-bedroom that had been painted about two hundred times, had no air conditioning, and had only a few cockroaches. It was in Forest Hills, Queens, at the corner of 62nd Road and 108th Street. To get to work, I would have to walk a few blocks, catch a bus to the subway station, take the train to 53rd and Lexington, and then walk three blocks to the Waldorf Astoria. My 50 percent increase was disappearing before my eyes. The subway ride was 20 cents, a shoeshine was 60 cents, and having a shirt professionally cleaned and pressed was 32 cents. Working at the Waldorf required crisp, white, starched, perfectly ironed shirts.

The upside was that I had a good position in the most famous hotel in the world. I was expected to look like a million bucks and wear nice dark suits, pressed shirts, cuff links, and polished shoes to look the part of a Waldorf employee. One had to look the part whether one could afford it or not.

The job turned out to have pretty much the same responsibilities as the one in Chicago, except that I was in charge of purchasing and receiving for food and beverage as well as the storerooms for issuing the products. I also had a much larger staff to worry about. I learned a lot about foods and their costs, along with other products I'd never seen or heard of before. The wine and liquor selection in the Waldorf was huge.

Fortunately, I had learned the importance of getting off on the right foot with the food and beverage director and the executive chef. Those two people were very powerful, and if I did not do my best, my career would be dead in the water. I was not about to repeat the mistakes I had made in Chicago. If you make a mistake, it's one thing, but if you repeat the mistake you're a fool.

I got off to a great start. There were a lot of control problems in the food and beverage department, so I had an opportunity to make a difference, and I did so. I worked hard six days a week. My day off was Thursday. I was living two lives. I looked like a million dollars at work and was as poor as a church mouse out in Queens. By then I'd been working for almost five years. Yet I was still not making as much money as I did as a banquet server. And I was living in the most expensive city in the United States, with a baby and a wife to provide for. Daniel was eating nine jars of baby food a day. I thought, *I can't afford this. Having clean shirts alone is costing 32 cents a day.* I would leave Priscilla $6 in cash on the counter every morning. We did not have a credit card. We spent only what we could afford. Six dollars was our daily budget for nine jars of baby food, my shirts, and everything else, including our food. I thought, *Why did I get into management?*

We sold our car when we moved to New York for two reasons: because we could not afford to keep it, and because five hundred cars a year were stolen in the ten square blocks we lived in—and we lived in a fairly nice neighborhood. We definitely could not afford to rent a garage, and certainly couldn't afford the high cost of car insurance. For the next three years, all of our outings on my day off were to places we could get to by subway, or someplace in the neighborhood. Without a car, Priscilla's days were busy just taking care of our family needs.

Almost every Thursday, on my day off, I would let Priscilla sleep late, and I would take Daniel to the Waldorf Astoria. We'd have breakfast at Oscar's Restaurant and then go to Central Park. When you work six days a week and get home late, you really have to cram in that special family time.

I learned a lot about food in New York, and at the Waldorf in particular, but we could only afford cheap restaurants on my day off, if we could afford to go out at all. It seemed that most ethnic restaurants were pretty cheap, so that's where we ended up eating. We definitely could not afford a babysitter, so Daniel went everywhere with us.

My boss at the Waldorf, Gene Scanlan, turned out to be my first real mentor. A mentor, to me, is someone who knows you and really wants to help you and teach you. Mr. Scanlan, as I called him, sat me down on day one and told me the rules for working at the greatest hotel of them all. I learned that every head of state, every queen, and every king who had ever come to New York City had stayed at the Waldorf. During meetings of the United Nations, the hotel was literally full of dignitaries, and with them came massive amounts of security.

The rules were simple:

You work six days a week. Your day off will be Thursday.

You never wear a brown suit or brown shoes after 5:00 p.m.

We will buy you a tuxedo, a white shirt, a bow tie, suspenders, and cuff links.

Anytime there is a black-tie event in the hotel, you will wear your tuxedo. You will not take your tuxedo home. You will keep it at work so it is always here when you need it.

You will need to check the events every day to make sure you are dressed properly during the day and in the evening.

You will always look well-groomed; you will always have clean, well-trimmed fingernails and polished shoes.

You will not have tattoos or piercings that anyone can see.

You will not have long hair or hairstyles or colors that are not natural and professional.

You will not look or act weird in any way.

This was the Waldorf, and those were the rules, and the rules were very clear. I learned to really enjoy clarity. If you want people to know the rules, tell them what they are, and tell them what will happen if they do not follow them. Then they can make the decision to work under those rules or leave. If you're in the corporate world, look at the front page of the organization's annual report and see how the most successful people in your company dress. If you're in a small organization, look at the owner for clues about what works professionally. Never underestimate how much impact the way you look will have on your career.

I worked as the food and beverage controller at the Waldorf for about a year. I developed a good team, and together we improved the controls and processes. Then I was told that I was being promoted to the position of assistant food and beverage director and would be Mr. Scanlan's assistant. The new position turned out to require a lot of administrative work: working on kosher menus for the chef, recording daily the number of customers served and sales for the restaurants, ordering menus and supplies, and many other things of that nature. Most important, the job was the stepping-stone for me to become director of food and beverage operations at Hilton Hotels. Everyone in the food industry wanted that position no matter what it paid.

I received no increase in pay for the new promotion. The recession of 1970 had arrived, and we received no merit increases for two years. And I had basically no authority over anyone. The restaurant managers at the hotel's six restaurants knew a lot more than I did, and they pretty much took direction only from Mr. Scanlan. I learned that your title is sometimes bigger than your authority, but you probably don't want too much authority until you truly know what you're doing, so I was in a good place. I really liked my new business card with my name, title, and the Waldorf Astoria logo in gold.

Mr. Scanlan took me under his wing and brought me to every banquet and to every restaurant in the hotel, in order to teach me about the foods, beverages, and service. Every Monday night at 6:00 p.m., he took me and another young manager, Bill Wilkinson, to dinner and ordered different foods and wines, explaining to us how they were prepared and the history of the particular dishes. This was not eating dinner; this was a class. I would never have eaten a raw oyster if Mr. Scanlan hadn't made me. I later quit eating raw oysters and clams after Mr. Scanlan came down with hepatitis from them and was out of work for three months. I was sorry that he had to stay home sick, but during that time I had the opportunity to take on a lot more responsibility, so it was a good learning experience for me. He survived his illness and came back to work. He was healthier, and I was smarter.

Mr. Scanlan also took me to the best restaurants in New York City and involved me in special events. One night, we catered a charity event at the Cartier jewelry store on Fifth Avenue; we set up the buffets on the jewelry cases throughout the store. Outside catering is a tough business, and this case was a lot tougher than most because the security needs were monumental. I learned you really have to be organized to make an event like that a success. Checklists are a must.

Mr. Scanlan enrolled a good friend, Dennis O'Toole, and me in the Grossman wine seminar that started at 7:30 p.m. on Monday nights. He paid for it because he thought we needed to learn all about wines. I suppose it was somewhat like tuition reimbursement, which did not exist back then.

Mr. Scanlan always took a taxi home. On many nights he would say, "Come on," and he'd drop me at my apartment so I didn't have to ride the subway home. That subway ride normally took an hour; by taxi, I was home in fifteen minutes. That was a big deal on a Wednesday night. I learned that these little acts of kindness are important. We should all do them when we can.

I think what I learned most from Mr. Scanlan was that it feels good to help others. He really liked helping people get ahead. I could feel his generosity. Giving your time to help others is a really special thing because most of us don't have any extra time, or at least we don't *think* we do. If it's at all possible, be a mentor to someone. Your mentoring might make the difference in their career success. There are people all over the world today who attribute their success to Gene Scanlan because he shared both his time and knowledge with them. I hope I'm remembered the same way.

One day Mr. Scanlan told me to order pastrami and corned beef sandwiches with coleslaw, potato salad, and pickles from six different New York delis. He wanted to do a taste test to compare their quality with ours, to see if we could improve. I learned from that experience to always look for a better way. Always focus on improvement. No decision is ever final.

Of all things, we even had a buttermilk tasting at one time. I did not like that tasting, and I still don't understand how anyone can drink buttermilk. But I've tasted it because Mr. Scanlon made me do it. Not even my mother had been able to get me to do that. It was quite an experience.

I remember being assigned to create a menu for a special dinner that might have been served in the 1700s. That was the day I learned about fiddlehead ferns. This is not a big deal, but it does show that learning never ends. Mr. Scanlon taught me how to research menu items from different eras for special events. Today, with the Internet, that should be much easier. Go ahead and Google fiddlehead fern and you will learn something very few people know. You might even want to sauté some up for dinner tonight, if you can find them.

I had my first caviar and my first French champagne at the Waldorf, and I liked them both. I had my first martini in New York City, and I did not like it, but it was an experience anyway. Reading about foods and beverages and tasting them are two different things, as with everything in life. As I'll say many times in this book, experience matters, and in my opinion it's the best teacher of all.

I received a call in my office one evening to investigate a guest complaint in the Peacock Alley lounge in the Waldorf lobby. A guest thought the cocktail server was manipulating the guest check and overcharging them. I went down, approached the waiter, and asked to see all of his guest checks. I'll never forget how his hand started shaking as he took the Budweiser from his serving tray and smashed it into my right eye. Come by someday and I'll show you the scar from the six stitches I needed.

Until my son was old enough to know the truth, I told him that I'd gotten the scar falling down a flight of stairs. I did not want him to think his dad had been beaten up at work. I learned to approach future investigations with more caution and to have another person with me. I can tell you, however, that it didn't work out the way I had hoped the next time either. A few years later, I was hit by another waiter and fourteen more stitches were added to my head and the other eye.

New York City is a rough-and-tough city and a very diverse place. I think one reason I have so much appreciation and respect for diversity today is because of the years I spent in the hotel business with guests and fellow employees from all over the world. If you live in places like New York, you get exposed to so much diversity, from foods to cultures to religions, and on and on. In New York, you either appreciate diversity or you don't make it. I remember what a coworker at Disney told me one day when we were talking about diversity. He said, "In New York City, I was a CPA. In Orlando, I am a black CPA." In New York, it's all about performance and not where you are from, what color you are, or what religion you practice.

The Waldorf was a very intimidating place when I first got there, and I was really insecure. I experienced discrimination and bigotry because I was an Oklahoma college dropout country boy while most of the other managers were from the best hotel schools in the world. When I left the Waldorf for my next assignment and promotion almost three years later, I was very secure in my technical knowledge and my management abilities, and I had learned some excellent lessons in leadership from watching Mr. Scanlan and our executive chef, Arno Schmidt, in action. They were intelligent, nice, respectful, competent, and tough leaders in a hotel known around the world for excellence.

When it was time to leave the Waldorf, in 1972, I'd been working for a total of seven years, and I was not making the money I'd hoped to be earning. But I had earned $3 million in experience.

Next, Priscilla, Daniel, and I journey up to Tarrytown, New York, where I am finally in charge of something and ready to make my fourth million in experience! With that promotion came a salary increase. I was now making $14,000 a year—a thousand more than I'd made in my first year as a banquet server back in 1965, seven years earlier!

Insights

To get the job you want, be great at the job you have.

Even bad experience has value.

Make sure it's not your fault.

You own your experiences.

There is always a way to survive.

Be nice.

Get organized.

We all learn in different ways.

Establish and maintain comfortable relationships.

Be where the action is.

Be fair and firm.

Ask questions until you understand.

Skill is not enough.

Don't focus on your authority; focus on relationships.

Don't be afraid to apologize.

Learn the rules; clarity matters.

Economic recessions are part of the game.

Checklists work.

Situations can be tough; be tougher.

Connect yourself to great mentors.

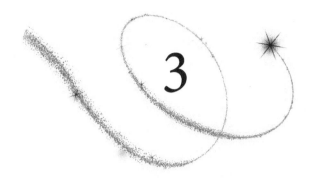

My Next Three Bossy Bosses: 1972–1973

It was 1972. I had been working for seven years. I had eight positions behind me. My family had relocated from Washington, to Chicago, to New York City. And now we were relocating once again, this time to Tarrytown, New York, about forty miles north of midtown Manhattan. I was leaving the Waldorf Astoria grandeur for a new role in a 205-room Hilton Inn. I was to be the executive assistant manager and director of food and beverage.

I believed that the previous eight jobs and experiences had prepared me well for that position, where I would finally oversee my own department. I had learned to be a well-organized manager, and I'd improved my technical knowledge and expertise. But no one up to that point had even spoken to me about leadership responsibility, and I wish that my leadership behavior had been better. I recall a couple of examples that I will keep to myself. I wish someone had taught me more about leadership before I made some of those mistakes.

Later, in 1995 when I was working at Disney, all the years I spent making mistakes and observing both great leadership and poor leadership enabled me to develop the Disney Great Leader Strategies. If you want to know more about my leadership strategies, read my book *Creating Magic: 10 Common Sense Leadership Strategies from a Life at Disney* so you too can avoid these pitfalls.

We moved out of our seventh-floor Queens apartment overlooking the Long Island Expressway and the 1960 World's Fair grounds. It was the noisiest apartment I ever lived in. Priscilla and I used to imagine that the sound of the traffic was the ocean. Sometimes you really need to use your imagination to survive and to get some sleep. We had made only one big purchase in the three years we lived in that apartment, and that was a $35 window fan. It wasn't air conditioning, but it was a whole lot better than nothing.

Tarrytown, New York, on the other hand, is one of the nicest, prettiest places on earth, right on the Hudson River. This is the area where Ichabod Crane and the Headless Horseman were from. I often drove over the bridge that the fictional character rode over to terrorize people in Washington Irving's "The Legend of Sleepy Hollow." Back in Ichabod Crane's day, it was a wooden bridge, though.

We rented a nice garden apartment on the first floor with a good view of the woods. It really felt like the good life after being in New York City for three years. Plus, the rent was cheaper and there were lots of kids in the area. Even the name was good: the place was called Sleepy

Hollow Apartments. Of course, Priscilla and I knew that the Headless Horseman hung out in Sleepy Hollow, but we did not mention that to Daniel. We stuck to stories from Disney and Golden Books. He was into Mickey Mouse and Donald Duck, which were much more appropriate than the Headless Horseman at the age of three. It was his third move since he was born, but at that age, kids couldn't care less as long as Mom and Dad are around.

My only day off was still Thursday, but now we lived only about half a mile from the hotel, so one of my perks was no commuting. That was a very good thing because we didn't own a car. Remember, I said that every job has things that are good and things that are not so good. I have a name for this, which I will tell you later.

Within two weeks of moving to Tarrytown, however, we realized we had to buy a car. Living out in the country, Priscilla could not go anywhere without one. My $3 million worth of experience was not much help in buying a car, and with my salary we could not afford a good, reliable vehicle. I ended up buying an old Opel Kadett from a manager who reported to me. I paid $250 for that car, and it was on its last legs—more on that mistake later.

You would think that with the impressive title I had at that time I would be rolling in dough. In fact, we still lived from paycheck to paycheck. Hilton did not even offer a medical plan back then. When we got sick, we paid out of pocket. For instance, when Daniel was born, in Chicago's

South Side at the now-closed Michael Reese Hospital, it cost us $1,200. That money came right out of our pocket.

But I found the Tarrytown job exciting. I was finally in charge of something. I quickly found out that being in charge brings on lots of stress, coupled with long hours. People actually expected me to make decisions and to know what I was doing. The guests, too, always wanted to see the person in charge, which was me, and 99 percent of the time they were not happy.

We performed three hundred-plus weddings a year at the hotel. These were upscale events, attended by local people who were wealthy and demanding. They did not understand the word *no*, so I had to find alternatives that satisfied them. I had no choice but to look for clever alternatives and to improve my diplomatic and negotiation skills.

I remember one father telling me that if anything went wrong with his daughter's wedding I would be receiving lots of flowers. He was a florist. I knew what he meant: that he would be sending flowers to my funeral if his daughter did not have a perfect wedding. I did not think he was joking! I made sure I was on duty that Saturday night for the wedding. Sometimes, excellent performance is literally a life-and-death scenario.

The hotel also had the most popular restaurants in the area for special-occasion dining. We had to be great. We had no choice because our guests demanded it. Some of them came up from New York City and Long Island on weekends during the summer months to stay at our Cabana Club. They were rich, tough, and demanding.

I learned a lot dealing with unreasonable people. I always looked after their needs and never let them see a hint of a poor attitude in me. I thought a lot of negative things, but I never expressed them to anyone. Lesson: *Know your role and know your part, and then perform it perfectly.* This is also called professionalism.

I worked the dining room every Friday and Saturday night, helping my restaurant manager handle special requests from guest after guest. Many times, I was in the kitchen helping the executive chef plate up a banquet or even peel shrimp. Small places do not have a lot of extra help when employees call in sick. My past experiences as a server and cook were helpful on those busy nights. I actually knew what I was doing, and the staff appreciated my help.

We knew at the Walt Disney World Resort that frontline cast members expect their leaders to know the jobs those cast members do and be able to perform them. This is a good lesson for everyone. Can you do the work of the people you lead, or at least know how difficult it is, emotionally and physically?

One day, I even had to drive around the Westchester County country roads to find a stand that sold vine-ripe beefsteak tomatoes because one of our guests was demanding them for dinner that night. I found them.

One night, the kitchen was so hot that we could not get the whipping cream to thicken. We ruined the entire batch of whipping cream we had on hand trying to whip it. So I raced off to a local restaurant to borrow two quarts of cream, and then to my apartment, where Priscilla whipped it up for us. Then I sped back to the hotel and, without a moment to spare, walked right into the dining room with the bowl in my hands and served the cream right onto the fresh berries that were already in front of the guests. Living close to work and having Priscilla nearby really paid off.

At the end of the dinner, the host put something in my hand and said, "Thank you, Lee. That was a great dinner." It was a dollar!

I said, "Thank you!" Yes, we were allowed to take tips, and yes, he was serious. Even back then, a dollar did not go far. If it had been $20 I would not have remembered it, though, and I would not have a good story to tell you. Just this week, my grandson Jullian was telling me about a difficult guest who left him no tip after running up a $60 tab at the Chefs de France restaurant at Epcot, where Jullian was a waiter. The next guest left him an $80 tip and another left $100. The lesson: *Always take care of everyone equally and in the end it will all work out.*

The days were long in Tarrytown. While managing, I went to work around 8:00 a.m. and got home between 8:00 and 10:00 p.m. every evening, six days a week. Over the years, the more I was in charge, the longer the hours became. Then, in 1980, I took a time-management seminar. That changed my life. We'll get to that story soon.

Actually, I wasn't in charge as much as I thought I was. The guests were in charge! I learned that pretty quickly, and it was a very important lesson. Being in charge is not always as fun as it's cracked up to be.

Tarrytown Takeaways

I learned a great many things in that position. Things are different when you're the best hotel in town, especially when the town is small. The hotel had only 205 rooms, but our food and beverage sales were larger than in many thousand-room hotels. Because of all of the weddings and special events we hosted, we were one of the top hotels in the company for profit. That was a nice place to be.

In small places you get the opportunity—whether you want it or not—to experience every frontline position, and you get that opportunity daily. Because I had learned what was possible, I introduced new policies and procedures. For example, I installed home-size washers and dryers on each guest room floor and had the housekeepers wash and dry all the towels and washcloths every day and put them back in the guest rooms instead of sending them out to a laundry. Only the sheets went out to a commercial laundry to be processed. There are many things you learn to try, out of necessity, in small places. It also helped the bottom line immensely.

Even back then I was fascinated by motivational tapes and books on leadership and management. I bought a set of tapes on motivation and played the tapes for thirty minutes at my weekly staff meeting, followed by a discussion. I don't know whether or not my team really liked them, but I did, and I think they helped us gain a different perspective on the subjects of management, customer service, and leadership.

One good lesson is that you had better decide in advance what you stand for and know what ethical, honest leadership behavior looks like. One day, a man who owned a taxi company came to see me. He handed me an envelope and said, "All I want is for you to make sure that only *my* taxis are allowed to wait in front of the inn to pick up your guests."

I opened the envelope to find ten $100 bills—$1,000! I had never in my life held $1,000 in cash in my hand. I felt dizzy; my stomach and head were spinning. Priscilla and I did not have one dime in the bank. We needed a car badly. We needed a lot of things, in fact. I could think of a hundred ways to spend $1,000. If you think that's a lot of money today, just think of what it was back in 1972, when you could buy a new car for $3,000.

I took a deep breath and said, "Sorry. I can't do that," and handed the envelope back to the man. I knew what he was asking me to do was wrong, and I was glad that, long before that moment, I had settled on my own ethical standards for honesty and integrity. Make sure you have too. It's just a matter of time before you will find yourself in a delicate position in business or in your personal life. Know what you stand for and what you will not stand for!

- *What would you do today if someone offered you drugs at a party?*

- *What would you do if you had a chance to take a little money from the register at work—and you knew that others were doing it?*

- *What would you do if your boss told you to inflate the inventory this month to make the profit look better?*

- *What would you do if your leader showed you how to code an invoice as expense instead of capital to slip the expense through and then told you to do it?*

- *What would you do if you worked for Disney and your fellow employees asked you to use your Disney Pass to get their friends or family into the parks?*

- *What would you do if you knew that fellow employees were abusing their discount privileges on merchandise or food?*

You had better figure out right now where you stand. It's important to do the right, honest, ethical thing when you're confronted with these kinds of issues. The front pages of newspapers are full of stories every single day about people who have not prepared themselves for moments when their integrity would be tested. Some go to jail. Some humiliate their families and disappoint their friends. Some commit suicide. Some get divorced. There's nothing worse than having to share that aspect of truth regarding yourself or family with others.

Tarrytown is also where I got involved in United Way. I even ran the campaign in 1972. I didn't do it correctly, though. I had every employee fill out a United Way pledge card and sign it in front of me. We raised a lot of money, but I learned that many people don't appreciate that kind of tactic. Live and learn! I did not repeat that behavior when I ran the United Way campaign for Disney World and for central Florida many years later. In fact, I learned another good lesson from Michael Eisner, the CEO of The Walt Disney Company at the time. I asked him for a contribution to Orlando's United Way drive. He gave $100,000, and Roy Disney gave another $50,000. I wrote Michael a thank-you letter, but made the mistake of saying that we appreciated his contribution even though it was not that much as a percentage of his wealth. Before long, my secretary told me that Michael Eisner was on the phone and wanted to talk to me. I thought, *No way! Someone is pulling a prank.* But sure enough, Michael Eisner was on the line when I picked up the phone. "You made me feel bad saying my contribution was not very much," he said. "Lee, you need to learn to just say thank you when someone gives you money."

He was absolutely correct. In retrospect, I wonder: *What was I thinking? Was I crazy?* One hundred thousand dollars is a lot of money.

Onward to La La Land

I also had my first experience of not respecting my leader in that Tarrytown job. He did not make me feel special, or treat me as an individual, or respect me, or make me more knowledgeable. He was a screamer, and I can't stand that. After a year of having to deal with him, I lined up a job in another hotel company, in Dallas.

The top leadership at Hilton went nuts when I quit. They flew me to Chicago to meet at the corporate office with the executive vice president, Porter Paris. He put "full-court pressure" on me and talked me out of quitting. He made me feel special, and he promised me a promotion if I stayed with the company. I agreed, and he kept his promise. I was soon promoted to director of food and beverage at the thousand-room Los Angeles Hilton hotel. My salary was increased to $18,000 a year.

It seemed like the right choice and a great opportunity. Looking back, though, I realized I should not have stayed at Hilton. I'll tell you why a little later.

At that time Priscilla and I owned a good, reliable used car: a yellow 1972 Volkswagen Bug. I'd bought it for $2,000 from the general manager's secretary in Tarrytown. It was only a few months old. We drove that car for almost eight years and then gave it to my brother-in-law, Hank, who drove it for two more years before selling it for $400. That car cost only $160 a year to maintain over those ten years. It was a really good lesson in not wasting money on cars that depreciate immediately.

The Opel Kadett that only ran half the time I gave away to a local sheriff who used to come to the hotel for coffee. He was going to fix it up for his son. Poor kid! You would have to be a complete idiot to leave town in that car and go out on the interstate. When we owned it we stayed pretty close to home and kept within walking distance of a car-repair center. That's where our Opel spent most of her life. We still make wise financial decisions today. Priscilla has been driving her current car for seven years and drove her previous one for fifteen years.

In Tarrytown, I earned another million. I now had $4 million in total experience. But I kept thinking, *Is all this experience ever going to pay off in hard dollars?*

Our move to Los Angeles was exciting because neither Priscilla nor I had ever been to California. Hilton would not transport our car, so we hired a man we didn't even know to drive it to LA for us. I flew ahead to find an apartment. That yellow Volkswagen never ran the same after that 2,800-mile drive to our new home.

The downside to the move was immediate. We quickly realized it was very expensive to live in California. We could not find an affordable place near my job, a task made more difficult because, in those days, it was legal to deny apartments to families with children. We ended up way out in the San Fernando Valley. It took me an hour to get to work—even then the LA traffic was horrible. And we had only one car, so Priscilla had to go to the grocery store and other nearby places on foot, or by taxi in an emergency. We quickly made friends in our apartment complex with people who had two cars.

One thing was consistent, though: my day off was still Thursday. This proves that consistency is not always a good thing. Most Thursdays we would drive to Malibu or some other scenic place to have lunch and let Daniel run into the freezing Pacific Ocean. He was four, and when you're four the ocean is never cold.

We did have a nice new California-style apartment, which was expensive but somewhat affordable. The place we lived in was called Wishing Well Apartments for Children and Their Parents. I'm not kidding. If you were not fond of kids, that was not the place to live. Kids were everywhere.

I stayed in the job at the LA Hilton as food and beverage director for about a year. Once again, I had a boss I could not get along with. I promise it was not my fault. Plus, the general manager lived in the hotel and expected me to be there day and night. He too was a screamer. He was technically very good, but the word *leadership* was not in his vocabulary or his actions. He would not have lasted a day at the Walt Disney World Resort or at Marriott.

I worked very long and hard hours in that job: 8:00 a.m. to 8:00 p.m. six days a week. You can do the math. And I really didn't learn much. One thing I did learn in LA, as I had in my previous job in Tarrytown, was not to be like the people I reported to. I guess that was equivalent to some form of leadership training.

One upside was that I made a good, lifelong friend, Steve Kunis. He was a young catering manager at the time, and all these years later I'm still friends with Steve and his wife, Janice.

At one point, another good friend of mine, Helmut Horn, told me about a job in Lancaster, Pennsylvania, as the director of food and beverage at a privately owned hotel. The job paid 62 percent more than I was making in Los Angeles. So, because I was not able to save a penny and was totally fed up with my bosses, I decided to check out the possibility in Pennsylvania. The lesson I was about to learn was: *Don't make hasty decisions when you're in a poor state of mind.*

The Roller Coaster Plummets
The Big Career Roller Coaster was plunging straight down in a freefall at full speed. In the end, however, things turned out all right and Lancaster proved to be a key move, even though it played out differently from what I'd envisioned.

I flew to Pennsylvania and interviewed for the job. When I got home I told Priscilla I was going to take it. It paid $30,000 a year, $12,000 more than I was making in

LA. She surprised me; she said she thought I was making a mistake, adding that I should either get a contract or not accept the job.

I told her I knew what I was doing. We were going to Lancaster. I figured having two bosses in a row with whom I did not get along would not get me much support for future positions at Hilton, especially since both of those bosses had been with the company for more than twenty years and I'd been around only eight. Plus, they were executives and I was not. My philosophy was "When they don't love you, or you don't love them, it's time to move on."

So I divorced them. I guess you could call it a corporate divorce. The number one reason people leave their jobs is that they don't feel appreciated. I did not feel appreciated.

So off we went to Lancaster in our yellow Volkswagen. It was our fifth move, and Daniel was only four years old. We found a great apartment that was much cheaper than what we'd paid in LA, and I was making a very good salary. I felt that I had finally made it. All of that experience had paid off at last. Priscilla was wrong and I was right: I'd told her I knew what I was doing, that I'm always right, and Lancaster was the right move.

I was fired ninety days later—with no notice and no severance pay. I was called in at 5:00 p.m. and was told "You have not made progress fast enough. You're fired." The whole meeting took less than two minutes. At 5:02 p.m. I was unemployed.

I was stunned. I had worked for ninety days in a row without a day off trying to turn the place around financially. I had not been told in the interviews that the company was almost bankrupt and on a cash-only basis for purchases.

So much for taking a job for the money. I'd now had three bosses in a row who had not treated me right. All three were good managers but, in my opinion, poor leaders. In the years I worked at Disney World, I would get calls from former cast members who wanted to return. They had been misled by promises from the companies they'd left Disney to join. The grass is definitely not always greener; it often turns out to be brown. That's a really good thing to remember. Be careful in your future interviews. And if you think things are bad where you are right now in your career, read on!

I had to face it: I'm *not* always right. I went home to tell Priscilla she'd been right all along. When I told her I'd been fired, she said, without hesitation, "Good. I don't like it here anyway." There were many other things she could have said.

I married a saint. She never once said, "I told you so. I said you were making a mistake. I told you to get a contract." It was a great lesson for me, and one you should pay attention to. She may have thought those things, but she didn't say them. She has always stood by me these last fifty-four years, and I've done a lot of stupid things . . . well, a couple at least.

Priscilla did have great role models growing up. Her dad, Charlie, was an officer in the navy and her mother was an English teacher. They had moved twelve times before she met me, so Lancaster was her seventeenth move. Her dad ended up becoming a rear admiral, by the way, so at least the moves paid off for their family. Eventually they would for ours too.

At that point, I was twenty-eight years old, with a wife, a four-year-old son, car payments, and eight years of quality experience. But I had no job and no savings, and I'd burned my bridges at Hilton. The lesson here is: *Do not burn your bridges.* If you leave a job, leave in a professional manner and tell them you hate to go. Telling your boss you think he's a jerk and a poor example of a leader may not be the best strategy; someday you might want to come back to that company or receive a reference from them. The other lesson is to try to save a few dollars a month in case of an emergency.

We decided to hit the road and look for a job. We called United Van Lines and told them to pick up our furniture and put it in storage. They came a day later and picked up everything we owned except the car and our packed suitcases. It did not take them long, as we did not own much at the time. Then the apartment complex we were living in promptly slapped a lien on our furniture because we were breaking a two-year lease after only ninety days. The sheriff confiscated everything, and we could not get it back until we paid $2,000 to the apartment leasing company. That was not a good day.

Fortunately, I had bought a whole life insurance policy eight years earlier, when I was at my first job, and I'd made monthly payments on it. It had accumulated a $2,000 cash value. So, I sold the policy and got the lien removed. Now, even my backup whole life insurance cash-value policy was gone. Things did not look good. I was definitely in a personal recession that would head toward a depression if I did not get a job quickly. So we headed off in our yellow VW Bug to find one.

I learned a lot more from that experience than I wanted to, as you can imagine. First, I never thought it was possible for me to get fired. At the time, it was the worst thing that had ever happened to me in my entire life, except for when a senior girl in high school would not go out with me because I was a junior, and when Priscilla wouldn't go to lunch or dinner with me back in 1966 because she thought I had a bad attitude. Looking back, I can see how she might have gotten that impression. It took a year, but she finally agreed to go to lunch with me, and the rest is history.

The upside of getting fired was that it eventually led me to a better place. It's funny how things work out sometimes. I found out there is life after being fired.

The second lesson was that I'd never imagined people could be so tough. The third was that I now understood the legal ramifications of breaking a lease. I probably hadn't even read the lease before signing it; now I read every agreement and every contract very carefully.

Another difficult lesson I quickly learned is that when you're unemployed, most of the people you considered friends, and most of your former associates, don't return your calls and don't step up to help you the way you hoped they would. But while some you thought were friends turn out not to be, others become extra special friends in a crisis because they really come through. Remember the saying "A friend in need is a friend indeed"? We were in a big need back in 1973. Today, I go out of my way to help my friends and family when they really need me, no matter what they need.

And let me tell you, I was in need. When we left Lancaster, we drove to New York to see our friends Suzie and Alain Piallat. They put us up and fed us. I worked the phones every day looking for a job. Then we drove to Priscilla's parents' home in Mississippi, and they put us up. Thank God for family and real friends.

My father-in-law, Admiral Payne, took me out to lunch to give me some coaching and counseling on how to change jobs in a more organized and secure way. I'd always felt intimidated by him. It took me fifteen years before I could call him Charlie. It was a long lunch, and I came away with a good lesson. I'll never forget the crab sandwich I ordered and never ate. I just kind of lost my appetite while he was coaching me.

After that experience, I would joke with him that I thought he was afraid we might move in with him and Sunshine (my mother-in-law's very appropriate name)—and that for the rest of his life he would have an unemployed son-in-law in his home, lying on the couch watching television. I did not tell him that joke until years later, though. At the time, it would not have been funny. It did, in fact, seem possible.

He would become proud of me, however, and he told me so when he and Sunshine came to visit us in Paris just a few months before his death in 1993.

I got up every morning and worked the phones. One day I finally made contact with someone I remembered from my time at Hilton in Chicago, Bud Davis. We did not know one another personally, but we each knew about the other. I knew he was great, and he told me that he'd heard I was too. My good performance at Hilton was about to pay off. Bud had since moved to Marriott, which was then a small, unheard-of hotel/motel company with thirty-two properties. My friends in the hotel business told me not to join such an obscure company because it would never amount to anything. Boy, were they wrong. So much for their advice!

In my previous three jobs I had really earned $4 million in experience. But I still had no real income and no savings. I did have my family, though. I can't even imagine how I would have gotten through that period without my family being there for me and having faith in my ability. It was 1973, and the United States was about to go into a two-year recession. It was not a good time to be looking for a job. It was bad enough having my own personal depression, economically and mentally, without the United States having one too.

Years later, my mother-in-law, Sunshine, needlepointed a pillow for me that said, "Behind Every Successful Man Stands a Surprised Mother-in-Law." She is so nice that she asked Priscilla if it was okay to give it to me. I always wondered if my getting fired gave her the idea for that pillow. She once told me that if I had not married Priscilla, she would have adopted me. Now that is pretty cool. Later on, I put a brass plaque on a bedroom suite in our home. It read "Sunshine Suite." She loved that.

In the next chapter, I'll tell you about the career rebuilding process when things do not go quite the way you had planned or hoped. Things that go up might come down, but they can also go back up if you stay focused and positive and learn from your mistakes—plus, look at all the great stories I have now.

Insights

When it's time to go, go.

Always say thank you.

The cost of living is often the cost of learning.

Bad decisions can turn out for the best.

As Seen In The Main Street Leader

Promises, Promises, Promises.

Do You keep your promises?

Great leaders keep their promises. Every day, leaders make explicit and implicit promises by the dozens. When you are someone's leader, it's expected you will do what you say and do what is expected of you.

Promises look like the following to people in your life:

"I will call you back on Friday."

"I will check on your costume and get back to you on Wednesday."

"I will make sure a crib is in your room when you arrive."

"I will be home no later than 7, or I will call you."

"I will make that change on your schedule."

You can find out how good you are as a promise keeper by talking to your peers, direct reports, and customers. Check your performance reviews. The answers are there, waiting for you to discover them.

Are you disorganized? Undisciplined? Are you leading by the seat of your pants?

If you are (and most people know if they have this problem), read my book *Time Management Magic*. Better yet, take the *Time Management Magic* course in the Cockerell Academy.

Do it now. Order the book or begin the course before you forget...

...and speaking of forget...never use this word again.

The word "forgot" really means...I don't care.

I forgot Valentine's Day in 1969, and my wife, Priscilla, has never forgotten it. And I never forgot it again.

My boss never heard me say, "I forgot," because I never said it.

Do you believe those people on the witness stand who say they forgot?

If you have this flaw, it can be hazardous. It can ruin your career and relationships. It hurts you, and it hurts the people who depend on you.

Is there anything more important for leaders than credibility?

Do what you say you are going to do.

It does not matter how much you know and how smart you are if you don't get it done.

Remember, paper and pencil were invented for a reason.

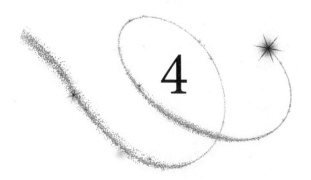

Starting Over: 1973–1979

So there I was, in 1973, recently fired, unemployed, and living with my mother- and father-in-law. But, as I said earlier, I was finally able to get in touch with Bud Davis, who had moved from Hilton to Marriott as vice president of food and beverage. I called him, and he asked me to drive to Marriott headquarters on River Road in Washington, D.C., for an interview. I had that interview with Bud and some other executives, and then took a leadership and management profile test called the Wittrick. It was a psychological test to determine if I would fit well in Marriott.

The "Wittrick test" no longer exists, but there are plenty of others out there, and you'll probably run into them when you apply for positions. Organizations today not only want to know what you know but how you think, how disciplined you are, what kind of judgment you have, how much empathy for others you have, what kinds of relationship abilities you have, and so forth. They want to know not only what you can do but also how you will do it.

One thing my Wittrick test pointed out, probably not the best thing, was that I had problems with authority. That turns out to be true. I'm not too fond of people telling me what to do and using their authority to push me around. I have seen many people abuse their authority in all walks of life, from parents to bosses to law enforcement. My reactions have gotten me into problems from time to time in the course of my career. That's probably why I quit two jobs and had run-ins with some of my bosses. I don't have a problem with a boss I respect and who sets a good example, respects my opinions, and involves me in decisions affecting my work. But I do not work well with, or react well to, bosses who can only get results by exercising their authority. This is the classic behavior of bullies. I have a basic distrust of people in positions of authority. Maybe I need to get counseling to overcome this problem. At age seventy-seven it might be a bit late for that, even though a favorite quote of mine is "It is never too late to get better."

I guess I passed the Wittrick test because Bud called me and said, "Lee, we have the perfect job for you in Philadelphia as a manager." The title was "complex manager," which included responsibility for two restaurants, a bar, room service, and food and beverage operations at the swimming pool. It paid exactly what I'd earned back in Los Angeles a few months earlier. The lesson here: to make more money, you usually have to stay employed where you are. Remember, I had a higher salary in Lancaster, but I was fired after ninety days so my annual salary for all of 1973 was lower than what I'd made before I left the Los Angles Hilton.

There was one fabulous benefit, which I did not appreciate at the time. Marriott awarded stock options, even to people at my level as a complex manager.

I threw them in a drawer at home and forgot about them because I had no idea what a stock option was. As it turned out, they had a huge value only a few years later; in fact, they paid for Daniel to go to Boston University for four years and for Priscilla to get a really nice diamond ring we could finally afford after all of those years of marriage. Factoring in the stock options, my income actually went up dramatically, even if I didn't realize it at the time. I was just happy to be employed again.

One of the first things I had to learn was what "complex manager" meant. I wondered if it was actually the job title or stood for the required personality of the person in the position. I think it's best to label positions with terms that can be identified with the jobholder's responsibilities. I'm sure that not one single guest understood that title on my name tag.

I told Priscilla the potential job was in Philadelphia. She said, in an alarmed voice, "Philadelphia!" We had never been there, and for some reason we had a negative opinion of the city. Maybe we had watched too much television. It turned out to be one of the best places we ever lived. As they say, "Home is where the heart is." And your heart is usually where your family is.

I drove to Philadelphia for a second round of interviews with the Marriott's general manager, Dick Stormont, and the director of food and beverage. I found out later that after my interview, they both recommended that Bud Davis not hire me. They thought I was too quiet in the interview and did not show much enthusiasm. They said I was "too low-key." Actually, believe it or not, that became my nickname at Marriott for several years: "Low-Key Lee."

My philosophy in those days, which suited my introverted nature, was to let my résumé speak for itself. I really did not know how to sell myself. Over the years, I learned to tell people:

- *What I can do for them in great detail*

- *What my strengths are*

- *What they can expect from me*

- *What my weaknesses are*

I was a real introvert early in my career and terrified of public speaking. I just quietly did my job. I'll tell you in a later chapter the downside of being a poor public speaker when you're in a leadership position, and why being too low-key can be misunderstood (although you don't want to be a bragging loudmouth either).

I am a closet introvert, but I learned how to act like an extrovert. This can be done, I discovered, through courses, reading, and practicing. The main reason I'm more extroverted now is that my self-confidence and self-esteem grew as I had more and more successes in my life.

One thing to remember is that if you're not good at something and that thing is important to your future, it's simply something that needs to be worked on before it hurts you or your career.

You probably already know what you need to work on, so don't be afraid to ask for feedback and help from people who know you well and will both encourage you and tell you the truth.

Being able to communicate and speak in public is important in any leadership position. Leaders spend a lot of time influencing others through communication and personal example. If you're unable to explain clearly what you believe in and what you want people to do, you'll have limited success in leading them to the results you're trying to achieve. Most people are more afraid of public speaking than they are of death. Death can't be avoided, but being a poor communicator can. We'll talk more about that a little later.

In any event, I got lucky after that Philadelphia interview; Bud Davis exercised his authority and told them to hire me. I didn't know that until years later, or I probably would have been even more insecure than I already was. I must admit I had to eat some humble pie in that job. It was not the same as my earlier position as director of food and beverage at Hilton. I had also recently been fired, and that takes quite a lot of arrogance out of you, so I had to take it down a notch. I'll tell you, though: eating humble pie is better than not eating at all, and it turned out to be one of the best things that ever happened to me. By taking the position in Philadelphia, I gained a lot of experience I really needed. I hadn't had the opportunity to gain that experience earlier, and it would serve me well in the future.

Before reporting to my new position, I was sent to the Boston Marriott for a month of training. At the time, this was the benchmark hotel in Marriott's food and beverage systems and food quality. Unfortunately, relocation policies back then were not what they are today. Priscilla and I were expected to find our own accommodations and to pay for them ourselves during the month-long training period. This, we quickly found out, was impossible.

I called Bud Davis and told him my hard-luck story. He made an exception to the policy and put us up in the hotel. My meals would be covered, but not Priscilla's and Daniel's. We were so poor that we would order a cheeseburger platter and share it. I know you might find that hard to believe, but it's the truth. Relocation policies have come a long way since then.

Up until then, 1973 had been the worst year of my life. But it would turn out okay eventually. In fact, it would be a key year in my career. It was a rebuilding year of sorts, and I learned many lessons that I would not soon forget when faced with future decisions.

The training in Boston turned out to be great. I learned a lot, and the director of food and beverage, Olaf Arnheim, took a personal interest in my training. I was very fortunate to train under Olaf. He had been with Marriott since leaving college and was a true expert in the food and beverage business. He had especially strong management skills and was both very well organized and extremely candid. One always knew where one stood with Olaf. He was a great coach for me. Because I respected him as a leader, I wasn't bothered when he was brutally honest with me.

After my training, the three of us headed to Philadelphia in our yellow Volkswagen Bug to report to the new job. We found an apartment that we could afford in Phoenixville, Pennsylvania, nine days before Christmas, 1973.

Onward to the City of Brotherly Love

It was a good Christmas because I finally had a job and I was so glad that 1973 was about to end. "Thank you, Santa! I promise to be good this year" was all I could think of! I made several New Year's resolutions on New Year's Eve.

One of the great perks in the new job was that it was a five-day workweek. The expectation for management at Marriott was five ten-hour days. It seemed like those ten hours a day were harder in food and beverage than in any other department, but having two days off was fabulous. It's interesting what can make a person happy in life.

When I moved to having Sunday and Monday off after working six days a week and every holiday for the previous eight years, I was sure I'd have Thursday withdrawal. Priscilla and I had never spent a New Year's Eve together—or any other holiday for that matter—in the five years we'd been married. Because I was not around much in those years, Priscilla became the neighborhood babysitter wherever we lived. I think some people thought she was divorced.

Food and beverage professionals miss a lot of neighborhood parties and are always late to family gatherings. Actually, I lost track of the time between when Daniel started to walk and when he started to talk. I regret that, but he turned out all right thanks to his mother being there to keep an eagle eye on him. I've made up for it by spending lots of time with my grandchildren, Jullian, Margot, and Tristan.

My new position turned out to be a great experience. I had never managed a group of restaurants like those before. The restaurants were very busy, and Marriott's service standards were very high. Those were the days of the salad bar and lobster or prime rib dinners for $5.95. The 1973–75 recession triggered such high-value, complete-dinner concepts to drive business into hotel restaurants. Almost every restaurant had a salad bar in those days. The simpler food production and narrower menu selection also reduced labor costs.

Many good ideas are born out of recessions because you're forced to try new things. Recessions are great at breaking down resistance to change. If you're resistant to change in a recession or a business downturn, you're usually not employed by the time it's over. Great leaders support and drive continuous improvement through their own personal example, often having to push through the resistance they encounter. They often stand alone when quick and decisive change must happen. That is why they say "It is lonely at the top." There are only two reasons people change: education or crisis.

I was also in charge of the kitchen, and the chef reported to me. She had been with the company for forty years. I did not order her around. Her nickname among the employees was "Mom." Her real name was Helen Malishka. You do not order people around when they're called Mom, especially when they know a lot more than you do and they *know* they know more than you do. Mom took me under her wing and taught me a tremendous amount about food production, sanitation, proper storage, dating, rotation of food, proper cooking methods, and safety, both in food handling and in work habits. Remember, you can develop your boss if you do it with finesse. Mom did a great job training and developing me.

One thing that stays with me is the Marriott concept "Clean as You Go!" This basically meant that everyone kept the place clean. If you were a cook and dropped an eggshell, you picked it up. The kitchens and the kitchen floors were spotless and always kept dry. Marriott's accident frequency was half that of every other hotel company. We could all learn from this sort of simple but clear rule. The employees met the expectation because there were consequences for not keeping the place spotless and safe. Lesson: *Be clear with your employees, and they will deliver for you.*

In that position, I learned to have strong processes and checklists in place, and to make sure no one went home at the end of their shift before their work was completed. Back then, as today, we would have visits from executives from time to time, including Bill Marriott, the CEO of the company.

Everyone would run around saying we had to get ready for these VIPs. I made a policy of never saying or doing that. I made sure that our areas always looked good and that we were ready for anyone at any time. I just did not like the concept of getting ready for an important visitor. It seemed to be dishonest and very manipulative. I often heard during my time at the Walt Disney World Resort about managers who would tell their fellow cast members to get ready for someone, like Michael Eisner, Bob Iger, Al Weiss, and even little old me. What they were really telling people was to cover up and make things look better than they usually were. I just made sure that I or one of my managers checked out all our employees before they went home to make sure they'd completed their work properly. In that way, we were always ready!

When I was first put in charge of park operations at Walt Disney World, I visited one of the attractions at Epcot. I later heard that the manager on duty was afraid it looked as though they were overstaffed, so he quickly asked some of the cast members to stay in a closet until I left. Isn't that the most bizarre and silly thing you ever heard? This may be an urban legend, but I've heard it many times over the years. I hope it wasn't true.

At one point, long before electronic clocking in and out was invented, I carried the time cards in my back pocket. When employees wanted a break, they came to me. When they returned from their break, they gave me their card back, and when they were ready to go home, they came to me to say goodbye. I would check out their work area before giving them their time card so they could clock out and go home. No one was able to slip out without doing his or her work; therefore, we were always ready. Eventually, I did not have to check their work any longer or hold on to their time cards because they knew what I expected and they met my expectations, knowing I would check.

Another perk in my new job was that it was a bonus position. A big factor in how my bonus was calculated was accident frequency. That got me and everyone else focused on safety. More about this a little later.

The importance of expectations and consequences was one of the important lessons I learned at the Philadelphia Marriott. I learned that from Bill Marriott himself. One day, he said, "Lee, the only way you get excellence in any organization is through education and enforcement. Most leaders do okay with the education [training] part but fall flat on their faces when it comes to enforcement [discipline]."

I was also taught how to coach and counsel employees at that job. We were given extensive training on the subject. We had no union, but we had what was called the "Guarantee of Fair Treatment" policy. It was the leadership's responsibility to coach, counsel, and discipline employees. The coaching had to be documented and put in writing. If an employee felt he or she was being treated unfairly, the employee could go to the next level, all the way up to the president of the company, Mr. Marriott himself.

Being able to coach and counsel people was a wonderful thing to learn because it's for their benefit. Doing the coaching, counseling, and disciplining immediately after the employee has done something, either right or wrong, was one of the greatest lessons of my life. I also learned that good coaching involves giving employees the appreciation, recognition, and encouragement they deserve. Remember, the number one reason employees leave a company is that they don't feel appreciated.

Today, I think that most people who worked under me would say that I didn't order them around. I work with my team to arrive at the best solutions rather than compel people to do things. I do, though, use every ounce of my experience, teaching skills, persuasion abilities, and any other talent I have to make my point of view understood; then I listen to their point of view until we arrive at the right place. It's important not fall madly in love with your ideas before you've heard from others. Stay open-minded and flexible. I learned this working with "Chef Mom." I admired her a lot. I was the boss, and she was Mom. I listened to her and learned from her, and we became great partners. I learned that the title "boss" is not a great title unless you like being bossy. We need fewer bosses and more teachers in the world.

At one point, after I was in the position for about three weeks, I had not seen or heard from the general manager or the food and beverage director, and I was dealing with some very tough issues. The place was a mess. I told Priscilla one night, "I think I made the biggest mistake of my life taking this job." I was getting no feedback on my performance, and remember, I was a "recovering fired person." As a result, I felt very insecure. The very next day, I opened my mail to find a note from the general manager. It read:

Dear Lee,

> *I am sorry that I have not seen you since you started. I have been tied up in Washington working on some new projects.*
> *I just want to tell you that I am hearing great things from everyone about what a great job you are doing. We are really happy to have you on our team. You are making a difference.*

Sincerely, Richard

That day, I learned how important timely recognition is. That one note, which I have kept all these years, boosted my performance and my self-confidence, and self-confidence is one key thing you need to do your best work. Don't ever forget this lesson in every part of your life: *Building self-esteem and self-confidence is one of the most important things great leaders do.* Positive feedback is the fuel that drives performance. It's more powerful than the solid rocket booster fuel that was used to launch the space shuttles. And it's free, in abundant supply, and in great demand.

What a great fuel! I figured if I needed it so badly, others must as well. Fuel your team often so they can soar in their performance. In my first book, *Creating Magic*, Strategy 7 is titled "Burn the Free Fuel." I named that fuel A.R.E., for appreciation, recognition, and encouragement. This fuel changes lives, improves performance, and enhances the bottom line.

After about a year in that position, I received a promotion: I would now be director of restaurants. It was a bigger job in another part of the hotel. It included being responsible for a high-volume, twenty-four-hour coffee shop named the Fairfield Inn; a specialty restaurant steakhouse called the Sirloin and Saddle; a large live-entertainment venue, the Windjammer Lounge; and another, smaller lounge. I had responsibility for all food and beverage purchasing and controls.

I used all my prior experience to put in place a well-organized system for running the operation. I focused on putting in the right processes, operating guidelines, checklists, and controls. In food and beverage, tight controls are vital if you're to be profitable. The margins in that business are extremely challenging. Profits can literally be eaten up by employees if you don't have effective policies and systems and are prepared to enforce them.

I focused heavily on training. I insisted that managers always be on the restaurant floor and available to staff in case any problems came up. I set a good example for everyone by being out there in the operation myself when it got busy. I bussed tables, seated guests, and even washed dishes and mopped floors. I had learned the value of leading from the frontlines and not from the office.

I taught the managers how to do proper shift turnovers with a one-hour overlap so everything was in order for the shift that was about to begin. I established a policy that the manager going off duty could not leave until the manager coming on was happy with how the place looked and the way it was stocked. Shift-ending time for management was when all their responsibilities had been completed rather than a set time like four or five o'clock.

I put in place a monthly two-hour Saturday morning meeting. Every manager was required to be there, even if it was his or her sixth day. Without that meeting, the entire team would never have been together to work out operational issues and agree on consistent guidelines.

The twenty-four-hour restaurant served nearly four thousand guests a day, so being organized with staffing, equipment, and food production was critical. The job taught me a lot about how to organize for high volume and the importance of consistent guidelines for all employees. We used checklists for everything. To this day I still believe that a basic checklist on a clipboard is one of the most effective tools for keeping a business under control. Technology and computers are nice, but a good old clipboard and checklist are still my best friends. They never crash or need charging, and everyone can afford one.

All in all, I thought I was doing a very good job in Philadelphia. But I was about to learn that I was wrong about something. I thought I'd learned how to coach and counsel employees about their performance and behavior. As it turned out, it was not yet one of my top skills.

I had a longtime waiter named Roberts who caused a lot of disruption with other people in the organization. He was a real problem. I had spoken to him before, but in every conflict that arose, it was always his word against someone else's. He was very clever to not have any witnesses around when he said inappropriate things to other employees just to get a reaction from them and cause some trouble.

One day, he made a very disparaging remark to a Japanese cashier about her culture. She reported this to me in tears. Once again, there were no witnesses. But I was fed up at that point, so I called him into my office.

Remember the incident in New York, when the waiter hit me with the Budweiser bottle? That happened when I was alone with the guy, and one does not forget such things. So this time, I had Robert's manager come into the office too, just in case.

We sat down, and I reviewed with them the history of complaints I'd received from the man's fellow workers, just as I had done with him before. And, as before, he flatly denied that he had ever done anything wrong. He told me to prove it or shut up. I then made the mistake of putting my index finger about one inch from his nose and saying, "Mr. Roberts, you have a bad attitude."

He immediately reacted in a rage. He knocked me out of my chair. His manager and I ran out of the office toward the cocktail lounge to get away from him. He chased after us and hit me over the head with a clipboard that was hanging on the wall. This is the downside of having checklist clipboards hanging in your office. I now had fourteen more stitches, to add to the six I got in New York City.

I was right, of course. He did have a bad attitude. But being right is not always important, especially when you're bleeding from several places on your head.

That night, Priscilla said, "Lee, do you think this happens because of the way you talk to people?" I took that to heart, and it never happened again. I learned not to stick my finger in someone's face and announce my opinion of that person in such a straightforward, aggressive manner. I guess I was a slow learner about some things.

The Next Step Up

By that time, the country was in the middle of a major recession. It was the first recession that had affected me very much. Until then, I didn't really know what a recession was.

The one in 1970 had entailed not receiving a merit increase, but I'd never had to do mass layoffs before.

Now we had a recession where people were waiting two hours in line to get gas because of the fuel shortage. I quickly learned that a recession is when your sales are going down and you need to shed costs fast. You have to reduce costs as much as possible while attempting not to hurt your brand. Orders from headquarters came in, and we had to implement those orders immediately. We had to let go 10 percent of the employees, including management. Having to lay off so many people was a very difficult thing to go through. Putting people out of work at a time when you know they probably won't be able to find another job is extremely tough.

Soon, a new general manager arrived, and luckily for me it was Bud Davis, who had been instrumental in hiring me just two years earlier. Then, shortly after Bud's arrival, my boss, Hubert Roetherdt, director of food and beverage, retired.

I was sure I'd get the job. I was ready for it. I had the right experience, having been a director of food and beverage before, and my performance was highly rated. I was so convinced that there was no way I would not get the job that I was already thinking of how I would spend the extra income. I even told Priscilla I was going to get the promotion, and I think she told her mom and dad. But I would soon find out that the recession would affect me too.

Olaf Arnheim, who had trained me in Boston when I started with Marriott two years before, had moved on to a resident manager position at the Boston Marriott. In those days, that was usually the job people had prior to becoming a general manager. But because of the recession, the resident manager positions were eliminated throughout the company and the existing resident managers were redeployed.

It was announced that Olaf would be our new food and beverage director. I was really disappointed. First fired, then passed over. I was not enjoying it. I was not feeling special or respected. When I got to work the next Monday morning, Olaf was standing at the back dock door where the employee entrance was because it was also the security checkpoint. No employee was allowed to enter or exit the hotel any other way.

Olaf said, "Hi, Lee. I have two questions for you. First, how do you feel about me getting the job instead of you? Second, do you think you're making the right salary for your current responsibilities?"

Wow! Did that catch me off guard! I said, "I'm okay with you getting the job; and yes, I am paid properly." From that one experience I immediately learned to deal with issues that people are already thinking about, so you can put their concerns to rest and get on with the work. I love people who are candid and straightforward. I learned how to do this from Olaf.

A year later, Olaf was promoted to be the general manager of a Marriott hotel in Saddlebrook, New Jersey. This time, I was sure to be promoted to director of food and beverage. After all, I had been a good soldier. I had kept a good attitude. I had supported Olaf. I had been his right arm. I had achieved great business results. I had displayed patience. I thought Olaf trusted me, and now he and Bud would decide who would get the job.

I got the job!

There are many lessons to be learned from that experience. One is that success is a journey and not a destination. The additional year as restaurant manager was a drop in the ocean, looking back. It really did not affect my career at all, even though at the time I thought it was the end of the world. Patience really is a virtue. My positive attitude and support of Olaf are why he selected me to take his place. He trusted me, and that's why he recommended me to Bud as his replacement.

A year later I got a call from Bud. He told me he was leaving to be the opening general manager of the new Marriott on Michigan Avenue in Chicago, and Olaf was returning to Philadelphia as the general manager. That sounded great to me because I had a lot of respect for Olaf and was glad he would be my new boss.

Bud taught me a lot before he left. One big thing he helped me with was how to be less defensive. In those days, when I received some negative feedback on anything to do with my responsibilities, I would immediately go into battle stations and defend myself. I would give a million reasons why that particular assessment of me was wrong. I would explain exactly why I was being misunderstood. I took everything personally.

Bud told me that my eyes would turn red at those times, and my face would turn pale white as I focused only on defending myself. He would stop me and coach me and make me see how foolish I was being. Plus, he helped me understand how that kind of behavior would hurt my career going forward. I remember one day he called me and said he'd received a complaint from a regular guest that her tea was often cold. I immediately started to tell him all the reasons why that was not possible in my restaurant. He stopped me and said, "First of all, it's not your restaurant. And Lee, we're talking about cold tea. This is about the tea, not about Lee. The whole world is not about Lee. Go check to see if the cups and the water are hot."

Thank you, Bud Davis, for helping me with this behavioral problem. Today, I hate dealing with defensive people. And I'm still working on that insecurity myself. Being defensive, whether at home or at work, is not a good thing. It may be the biggest reason why some people do not get candid feedback from others. When you get out of control and overreact, people just quit communicating with you. Priscilla says I still have a ways to go in this area at home. I've learned that repeating the phrase "Let it go" over and over helps me react better when I'm getting feedback I don't like. Great lesson here! If you have this issue, just let it go, like Elsa did in *Frozen*. She was the queen, but she still had to learn not to abuse her position and her powers. My advice is to let it go, let it go, let it go!

Another thing Bud helped me with was pricing. I remember the day we raised coffee from 30 cents a cup to 35 cents, and a hamburger platter from $1.95 to $2.05. I could not imagine how we could go over the $2 mark for a hamburger platter. I was sure that none of our local guests would ever come back. I fought the price increase tooth and nail.

Bud said, "Lee, if you have great coffee and a great burger with hot, crispy French fries and fresh tomato, lettuce, and center-cut red onion with a nice big dill pickle—and you butter and grill the bun and salt and pepper the fresh meat—quality will win out." He was right. Our guest counts continued to increase, not decrease as I had worried they would. If you're famous for quality, then focus on quality. That was a great lesson I learned while working for Bud. It's not about the price; it's about the value. People ask themselves, *Was it worth the price I paid?*

Disney, Hilton, and Marriott have always known that quality will win out. Those three companies have been around for a long time and are still going strong. When you think of their brand, you think of quality. Price is what you pay. Value is what you get.

Back to the Windy City

The US recession eventually ended, but the city of Philadelphia had its own personal recession in 1976. It should have been a great year for business in Philadelphia as it was the year we celebrated the bicentennial of the signing of the Declaration of Independence in that city. It would have been a really big year for visitors, and all the hotels would have been full—only several people staying in a hotel in downtown Philadelphia suddenly died. They were diagnosed with a new disease caused by a fungus buildup in air-conditioning systems. It was named Legionnaires' disease because the hotel guests were attending an American Legion convention. Room cancellations began immediately after the deaths were announced, and Philadelphia found itself in its own little recession as people cancelled their visits in large numbers. Once again we were looking for ways to save, and having to reduce expenses and implement layoffs.

I had been working for Olaf for only a few months when he called me into his office to tell me that Bud wanted to talk to me about a new position: opening director of food and beverage at the Chicago Marriott.

This Bud/Olaf thing was working out pretty well for me. I couldn't believe that I'd be in charge of Marriott's biggest food and beverage operation at the time. Everything was going well. I was on a roll. Someone loved me again. Life was looking up. Being fired was becoming a distant memory. I was up to 80 percent in self-confidence, and my self-esteem was healthy. I knew I was offered the job because Olaf and

Bud had talked it over and agreed that I had both the talent and experience to do it.

As I've said, careers can be like roller coasters. When they're going up, things are smooth, fun, and calm—and when they go down, life is scary. Most roller coasters go up again after a fall, and yours can too. The difference between success and disappointment after a career stumble is usually the attitude you display and the tenacity you have to hang in there.

I talked to Bud on the phone. He knew me and I knew him, so I didn't have to be interviewed. Priscilla and I flew to Chicago on a Friday. We bought a house on Saturday. We went home on Sunday, packed, and moved.

Never buy a house that quickly.

It was our eighth move. It was 1977. Daniel was nine. I had been working for almost thirteen years. We had bought our first house in Berwyn, Pennsylvania, a suburb of Philadelphia. It was a small house. With repairs and having to sell it only two years later to make the move to Chicago, we ended up losing money on it. The only reason we could buy it in the first place was that my mother was willing to lend us the down payment, which I eventually repaid many, many years later.

We also had two Volkswagens. Priscilla's dad had bought a house in New York, and the owners had left a white Volkswagen in the garage. He gave it to us. We became a two-VW Bug family. The white one died after about a year, and we bought another one from one of my managers, Steve Bradley, who was being transferred to the Barbados Marriott. He gave us a really good deal on it because the *Philadelphia Inquirer* newspaper was on strike and he couldn't place an ad in the classifieds to sell it.

We bought a more expensive house in Chicago, and we lost money on that one too when we moved two years later. All the people I knew said they were making tons of money when they sold a house. It never happened to us. Looking back, I wish we had just rented for a little while longer.

The job at the Chicago Marriott was great. It was exciting to be doing all the planning, hiring all the managers, and working like a farm dog. The first six months were great because we were in preopening. The hard work started when we opened. And we opened big, with the National Restaurant Association convention. Every guest room, every restaurant, and every banquet room was full. Up to that point in time, 1978, it was the hardest job of my life.

Where did that five-day workweek go?

On opening day, I was invited to have breakfast with J. W. Marriott Sr., the chairman and founder of the company, along with his wife, Alice, the cofounder, and their son J. W. (Bill) Marriott Jr., the president and CEO, and his wife Donna. The name of the restaurant was Allie's Bakery, named after Mrs. Marriott (Alice). That was the last place I wanted to be on opening day.

I ordered a cup of coffee, and when the server brought the cream he stumbled and spilled the whole pitcher on Bill Marriott's brand-new tan suede jacket. In that half second, I saw my life flash before my eyes. I saw the light. I knew I was going to be dead.

Bill was very nice about it. He said something like, "Those kinds of things always happen to me. I think I make people nervous." That was the understatement of the day as far as I was concerned. But Bill had put me at ease—another sign of a great leader. I was back, I had seen the light . . . and I was back. My life had been spared. Whew.

While waiting for our food to arrive, I was lectured by Mrs. Marriott (Alice) on how to make a proper chili. She told me to always use pinto beans and never kidney beans. Then their food came; after a few minutes and a few bites of her breakfast, Mrs. Marriott turned to me and said, "Lee, if you don't fix the food in here I am going to take my name off of this restaurant." I saw the light again. I was dead for sure.

"Yes, Mrs. Marriott," I said. "Don't worry, I'll take care of it."

She said, "Okay, Lee, you do that. I know that opening day is difficult, but I want you to make this place great."

Once again, I experienced clarity with understanding. She was clear, and I understood what she wanted me to do. That is real communication. There was no misunderstanding on my part or her part. Ask yourself if you communicate with clarity, leaving no room for misunderstandings. This one thing will improve your performance and the performance of your team dramatically. Have the courage to tell the truth!

I was spared for the second time . . . I was given understanding. I was alive. I had not been defensive, and that worked to my advantage. I excused myself and went to have a heart-to-heart talk with my chef. You don't know what pressure is until you've had a day like that—and an opening day with the Marriott family to boot.

It was clear to me very quickly which leaders were competent and which were not. Everyone appears to be competent in the preopening period. But when guests show up, it's show time, and you find out quickly what everyone is made of.

I had never in my life fired a manager for poor performance, but I had to in that job. The first one I fired was someone with whom I had worked before and whom I had recruited and talked into leaving his old company to join me in Chicago. It turned out that he just could not get the place organized. His department was a mess, and he was in a key position. I put it off for too long, though, and one day Bud told me he was going to fire me if I didn't act. It was one of the hardest things I'd had to do up to that point in my career.

A few years later, when I took a time-management seminar, the instructor said one thing that put leadership into perspective: "A leader's job is to do what has to be done, when it has to be done, in the way it should be done, whether you like it or not." I love that statement and have never forgotten it. Even today, I think about it when I have to do something difficult. It even helped us in raising Daniel. I wish I had taken that course earlier in my career.

When I had to fire someone in those days, I would beat around the bush and tell the person at the end of an hour-long conversation that I had to let him or her go. At times I even blamed it on someone else, which is not the trait of a great leader.

After that, I learned to quickly tell people they're terminated and spend the next hour telling them why so they won't repeat their mistakes in their next position. I learned in the job that a big part of my responsibility was to deal with nonperformers and to think about all the people under them who were receiving poor leadership, not to mention the impact it had on our guests and the business in general. My job was not so much about the foods and beverages as it was about the people, their performance, and their leadership ability.

One Sunday morning in Chicago, I went to work after telling Priscilla and Daniel I would see them in a little while. I did not come home for six weeks. Priscilla brought me clothes and supplies and brought Daniel to visit me on the weekends. The problems at the opening were enormous. I had never before worked so hard. It's amazing how things can go from good to bad so quickly. At Disney, I used to call it going from magic to tragic in the twinkling of an eye.

It was kind of like 9/11. The day before, September 10, life was so good. I think those tough jobs over the years helped me prepare for what would lie ahead in my career. When you've worked in the food and beverage industry for a long time, nothing seems as hard as it would have been without those years of experience. An opening is also an experience everyone should go through.

I learned a lot about myself under the pressure. I learned that I could stay cool and calm, and that doing so had a calming effect on the rest of the team. I learned to spend time out and about, telling people how much I appreciated their efforts because, frankly, I was afraid they might quit. I learned how to be extremely firm and to give orders when I had to. You have to do this more during an opening, and during any crisis, than at other times in the cycle of a business, it seems. If you don't open right, the place never seems to run correctly afterward. I think that's what Mrs. Marriott was telling me at that breakfast, in her own unique way: getting it right quickly during an opening is really important.

Soon enough, we got organized and things started running smoothly. The only big mistake I made was buying that house an hour from the hotel, out in Wheaton, Illinois. The real estate agent told me it was only thirty-five minutes to downtown Chicago—true for Sunday mornings or at 3:00 a.m. but not when I actually had to drive to and from work. Plus, the snow and freezing weather added a whole other dimension to commuting. Do you know how bad a VW Bug heater is in a Chicago winter? You don't want to know. And, by the way, VWs had no air conditioning in those days, and I quickly learned that it gets really hot in Chicago in the summer.

Food and beverage employees have to be at work at all times of the day and night, and that commute caused me to leave work some nights before I should have and to sometimes come in later than I should have, just so I could see my family while I could still recognize them. The commute time was very stressful and disruptive to both my work and my personal life. After that, I always lived very close to work; my commute time was never again longer than fifteen minutes.

An extra two hours a day at home is a big deal. Too many people live far from their work so they can have a nice house and the so-called "good life." They say they do it for their family. That's great if you never want to see your family—or the house—during daylight hours.

Years later, when we moved to France to open Disneyland Paris, we remembered this lesson. We rented a 1,000-square-foot apartment on the east side of Paris so I could be close to work. The really nice, big apartments were on the west side of the city, but that would have added thirty minutes of driving time. It was tempting to get that perfect apartment, but I remembered the lessons of past openings. Thank goodness we made that decision, given the long hours I worked at Disneyland Paris.

Another major thing happened to me in that position in Chicago. Our director of marketing, Jon Loeb, asked if I would give a speech to three hundred convention delegates about the food and beverage business. I agreed. That was my first mistake because I didn't know how to give a speech. Remember, seventeen years earlier I had dropped out of my college speech class the day before I was required to give a speech. I was terrified.

I messed around for a couple of days and wrote out a speech on a yellow pad. I didn't really practice the speech, and soon the day arrived. I walked up on the stage and looked out at those three hundred people, and I knew right then that it was going to be a bad day. I read my speech, and you know how boring that can be . . . and it was. I rambled on. I really had no main points to make, and my lack of speaking experience showed.

It was an awful speech. I could see it on the audience members' faces. I knew they were thinking, *Get this guy out of here* and *What in the world is he talking about?* I didn't even know how to *stop* speaking, so I just kept blabbering on and on and on, hoping that if I spoke long enough I would have a heart attack and die, and I'd be out of my misery. To this day, my stomach hurts when I think about it.

The audience was polite. They clapped. But I knew the truth. The very next day, I began learning how to give speeches, how to make a point, how to be interesting, and how to use humor. The best advice I received was from Bill Marriott's father-in-law, Dr. Royal Garff, professor emeritus of speech and marketing at the University of Utah. He had taught speech and had written a book titled *You Can Learn to Speak!* He gave me his book and five pieces of advice. I have followed them ever since:

- *Do not give speeches . . . tell stories.*

- *Never give a speech about something you are not passionate about.*

- *Do not let people write speeches for you.*

- *Always use personal stories to make your point.*

- *Your audience does not know what you intended to say, so it doesn't matter if you forget something.*

That advice has worked really well for me over the years. Tell stories; don't give speeches—that was my main takeaway. I learned that once again when I joined Disney. Storytelling is the name of the game because everyone loves a good story and they remember them. I have since added one more rule to Dr. Garff's list: do not use PowerPoint. As I tell my clients, "Friends don't let friends use PowerPoint." I also tell them that my mother didn't use it. She would say, "Look at me when I am talking to you." It's impossible to be inspirational when you're using PowerPoint.

One day in late 1979, two years after we moved back to Chicago, I got a call from someone at Marriott headquarters in Washington, D.C. His name was Al LeFaivre, and he wanted to speak with me about a promotion to regional director of

LEE COCKERELL 111

food and beverage. He was the first important Al in my life. The second was Al Weiss, my boss at Disney World.

Al LeFaivre, regional vice president of Marriott Hotels and Resorts, had a background in marketing. He had checked into the Chicago Marriott without my knowledge and scoped out the food and beverage situation for three days to see what kind of operation I was running. He checked the food, the service, sanitation, maintenance, and many other things in all the restaurants, banquets, bars, and room service. He told me in the interview that he already knew how good I was. "Your operation is a reflection of *you*."

I never forgot that. Your annual performance rating cannot be higher than your operations performance.

One of the chapters in my first book, *Creating Magic*, recommends doing exactly that before you hire people: go check out their operation to see if they're as good as they tell you they are. In fact, they're only as good as the results they achieve.

I was about to leave Chicago for Washington, D.C., with $5 million in experience but still very little in the bank. Things were starting to look up financially, though.

We decided to give the yellow VW Bug to Priscilla's brother, Hank, who needed a car. We had been driving it for seven years. We took the white VW with us, or "the silver VW" as I called it when I used valet parking at a fancy restaurant. Asking for the silver VW always sounded better than asking for the white one. It was like asking for the silver Bentley or Rolls Royce.

I had now been working for fifteen years. I was thirty-five years old. Daniel was almost eleven and only seven years away from college tuition! Yikes! Priscilla and I still did not have much in savings. Living in very expensive cities had not left much for the old savings account or investments. Every vacation had been by car, and we stayed with family or friends because that was all we could afford. In those days, we could never have afforded a trip to Disney World.

Fortunately, I realized that I still had at least thirty more years to work, so maybe I was not in as much trouble financially and career-wise as I thought I was. Too bad we can't see forward as well as we can see backward!

Insights

Your reputation and your relationships matter.

Don't abuse your authority.

Locate where the opportunities are.

Identify and work on your weaknesses, skills, attitude, flexibility, and knowledge.

A demanding boss can be a good thing.

Strong procedures and checklists are vital.

Don't get ready for a crisis; stay ready at all times.

Education, experience, exposure = excellence.

Be humble, be teachable.

Be a teacher, not a boss.

Show appreciation, recognition, and encouragement.

Conversations and decisions can be hard, but they're the center of a leader's (and a parent's) responsibility.

Stay professional and your time will come.

Stay cool, calm, and collected under stress.

Get help when you need it.

The past prepares you for the future.

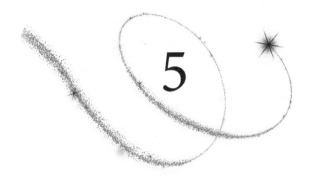

Nine Years of Promotions, Travel, and Disappointment: 1979–1988

The opening of the Chicago Marriott prepared me in many ways for my next position, at Marriott headquarters in Washington, D.C. It was November 1979. I had just finished my fifteenth job since 1964, and Priscilla and I were about to make our eighth move. She was happy because she'd grown up in Washington, D.C., and I was happy because I'd started my professional career there and I liked Washington a lot. Daniel, however, was not happy. He didn't want to leave his fourth-grade pals in Chicago. But he was unhappy for only about two weeks. If we all got over things as quickly as children do, we would be much better off.

My new role would be regional director of food and beverage operations for Marriott Hotels and Resorts for the East Coast. I would be working with a regional team of executives and would report to a regional vice president of operations. It would be my first executive-level position.

And we wouldn't miss the yellow VW Bug we gave to Priscilla's brother, because my new position came with a company car. As I pointed out earlier, every job has good things and things that are not so good. I also said I had a name for this. It's "perks and anti-perks." I sometimes think they cancel each other out. That car was a nice perk. The anti-perk turned out to be that I would be traveling just about every day and forced to be away from home Monday through Friday almost every single week.

Not having dinner with my family at night or breakfast with them in the morning was a difficult anti-perk. It was also tough because I was very tired when I got home on Friday evenings after barely catching the last flight from a northeastern city like Boston or New York in a raging snowstorm. Another anti-perk: the cost of housing and other things was quite a bit higher in Washington than Chicago. However, there was this big perk: my salary was quite a bit higher now. Perk, anti-perk, perk, anti-perk.

I had worked in operations for fifteen years. Now I was in a staff role at corporate headquarters—a completely different experience. I was part of a team made up of a regional vice president and directors of marketing and sales, finance, rooms division, human resources, and food and beverage. In that position, I did not have any official authority over the directors of food and beverage in the hotels up and down the East Coast. They reported directly to the general managers of their hotels. I was supposed to get my job done through influence and expertise. It turned out to be a bit of a challenge since my management style at the time was to get things done by telling people what to do and using my authority or intimidation to get it done.

At first I did not do as great a job as I should have in partnering with the general managers. I got better at it, though, because I figured out that I needed them on my side to get my job done. You see, no one had ever talked to me about leadership, partnering, and all the other things I would later write about in *Creating Magic: 10 Common Sense Leadership Strategies from a Life at Disney*.

Oh, how I wish I'd had that book back in those days. Much of what I wrote in *Creating Magic* was the result of my reflecting on both the successes I'd had and the mistakes I'd made along my career journey, as well as observing the behaviors of both great and poor leaders.

I was technically excellent, and I was an awesome manager, meaning I was organized and could make things happen. There were no deadlines I couldn't meet, and the people I worked with knew that. They also knew that they too had better meet their deadlines, whether they reported to me or not. I found out years later that my nickname was Doberman. Today I'm more like a cocker spaniel. I can bite, but I don't, and I don't even growl that often.

I completed my responsibilities as the regional director of food and beverage without fail. I got results, and I received the top rating every year on my annual performance review, which meant I received positive reinforcement for my management style. But I did it all by sheer drive and a touch of intimidation. I accomplish things quite differently today. This is the problem. If a person is not behaving properly and you give that person a top rating, then *you're* the one making the problem worse, and you're also hurting that person's future because bad behaviors always have consequences, sooner or later. Read the newspaper every morning. Every story is about failed leadership and bad leadership behaviors. Go ahead: get the paper and take a look. And don't look only at the big national and international news. These stories are in the local section too, and on the sports page, and definitely in the business section. I'm sure they're even in the classifieds. An entire cartoon series, *Dilbert* by Scott Adams, was inspired by poor leadership behaviors . . . and he will never run out of material.

In my new position, I traveled with a team every week to visit one or two hotels and audit their performance. We would check everything for compliance. We would invariably find many things wrong. These visits were very stressful for the hotels. When a Doberman approaches you, I'm pretty sure you experience some stress.

Later on I tried a different approach. I would tell the hotels thirty to sixty days before my visit what I was going to audit and check up on. That gave them time to get their act together. In those thirty to sixty days, they could adopt new operating guidelines and practices. As a result, the important things got done correctly and I would find things were right when I showed up. People learned from the process, and we were able to have good visits with far less stress. And before

I returned to a place, I would give the managers a list of different things to focus on.

By then, I was a mixed breed: half Doberman and half cocker spaniel. As the years went by, I gradually became more of a cocker spaniel and less of a Doberman. I transitioned from being a boss to being a teacher.

The lesson here is: *Looking for what is right is far more productive than only looking for what is wrong.*

Our team would sit together with the hotel management team at the beginning and end of the visit and decide on priorities. We would usually come back three months later and go over those priorities to make sure they were being achieved. We made lots of progress with this approach. We always left the hotels with a list of measurable priorities for them to work on accompanied by reachable deadlines.

Priscilla and I bought a house in Rockville, Maryland, a suburb of Washington, D.C. The recession of 1980 was in full gear, and interest rates were going up half a point a day because the recession had both runaway inflation and bad unemployment. The Federal Reserve was trying to get inflation under control before it dealt with the unemployment problem, so everyone felt the pain. I don't think Jimmy Carter was having a whole lot of fun over at the White House.

We finally closed at 11.5 percent on our mortgage and felt lucky at that, even though we'd had only an 8 percent mortgage back in Chicago. Unfortunately, a big portion of my salary increase disappeared because of those higher interest payments. It wasn't long before mortgage rates leaped to 20 percent. When that happened, our rate looked pretty good, but it was still in the category of anti-perk, as was the 7 percent local income tax in Montgomery County, Maryland. Real estate taxes were much higher as well, and so were many other expenses in the area.

One great perk was that we had stumbled into a really pleasant neighborhood, with good neighbors who had nice kids. I always learn a lot by watching the behavior of children, and I got a great lesson the day the moving van unloaded our furniture into our new home. The doorbell rang, and when I opened the door a group of little boys was standing there. The obvious leader of the group looked up at us and said, "Hi, I am Bobby Reiger. Do you have any kids?"

I said, "Yes, we do, but he's not here yet. He will be here in two weeks, as he is still in Chicago staying with his friends there."

Bobby said, "Okay, we'll be back!"

The lesson here is that if adults could learn to be as outgoing and direct, they would have new friends very quickly when they move to a new location. These kids were nine years old. To them, a moving van signaled the possibility of a new friend. To an adult, it signals thoughts like *I wonder who they are and if we will like them*, or *I wonder what he or she does*, or *I hope they are nice*. Kids don't wonder—they act! Today, thirty-eight years later, Daniel is still friends with James Toth, Arnie Pike, and Mark Surette from that neighborhood. We see them and their families often.

Another great perk was that the house we bought was nine minutes from my office in a great school district. The anti-perk was that I was usually not going to my office but to the airport, which was forty-five minutes away because of the infamously traffic-clogged Beltway in Washington. Priscilla thought it was a really great perk that Daniel could walk to elementary school, middle school, and high school. Yes, in those days, parents actually let their kids walk to school.

Priscilla's dad, Admiral Payne (Charlie), called one day and said he would like to give us his old company car, a four-year-old Chrysler. At the time, he was running a shipyard in Texas, having retired from a thirty-two-year navy career. All I had to do was fly to Dallas, pick up the car, and drive it back. It sounded good, and I did exactly that. We got rid of our last VW Bug. Plus, I received a good lesson on the drive from Texas to Washington. A Texas Ranger stopped me in the middle of nowhere. He came up to the car and said very politely, "Good afternoon, sir. May I ask if you have an emergency?"

I said, "No, sir."

"Okay then, you just sit right here while I write out your speeding ticket."

That officer was cool. His professional composure and the way he asked just one question impressed me. I wasn't even upset about getting the ticket. I'm sure that if I'd had a good reason to be speeding, he would have assisted me instead of citing me. The lesson is obvious: *Always stay professional.* He gave me the ticket and said, "Now you be careful and have a nice day." He was so nice he could have worked at Disney World.

Always remember that it's not what you say that upsets people so much as how you say it. Choose your words carefully. As my grandson Jullian reminded me, your tongue is one of the strongest muscles in the body. Be careful how you use it or you might hurt someone.

Priscilla now had a big car, and it was free. The anti-perk was that the car never ran very well. If it rained, it wouldn't start. And sometimes it wouldn't start when the sun was shining either.

One big thing I learned from having a job that required a lot of travel was to call home every night—but don't always tell your spouse what you had for dinner. We had great dinners on the road while Priscilla was at home trying to raise Daniel and often eating grilled cheese or tuna fish sandwiches. Great meals were a perk in the hotel business, and part of my responsibilities was to eat in the best restaurants in every city I went to. The anti-perk was my waistline growth if I wasn't careful.

Actually, I started working out regularly when I was twenty-seven. Being in the food and beverage industry, one can put on a few pounds each year before one knows it. I was actually jogging before it was commonplace and a cool thing to do. I was jogging before jogging shoes started to cost more than anything else in your wardrobe. Today, I weigh the same as I did when I got out of the army at twenty years old. I weigh myself every morning. I look up on the web how many calories I'm about to eat. I try to eat 400 or fewer calories for breakfast and another 500 or fewer for lunch. This leaves me enough room to have a nice dinner with some wine. I do weight training twice a week and walk or jog almost every day. That's another lesson for you: *Work out regularly.* Implement this habit in your life now! It takes a lot of energy to be a leader who has to work long hours. The difference between feeling good and feeling great is huge.

Another thing I learned was to make a reservation to take Priscilla out to dinner when I got home on Friday night instead of falling asleep on the couch and waking up just in time to go to bed. That kind of routine is really bad for a marriage, yet it's unfortunately practiced by many couples even today.

Managing Time

That year I received a memo from my boss, George Washko, saying I had to attend a mandatory time-management seminar. The seminar would last for two days, eight hours each day. I resisted and tried to talk my way out of going. I said, "I don't have time to go to a two-day seminar on time management."

That is the wrong thing to say to your boss about the subject of time management. If you don't have the time to take the seminar, then you probably really need it. It's like saying you don't have time to work out and stay fit; the end result is an early departure from this life.

One reason I resisted going to that seminar was that I thought I was already well organized. I got my work in on time, and I always received a great performance rating.

It turned out to be the best seminar I ever attended. What I learned was unbelievable. I think it was a key that has made a huge difference in my entire life ever since 1980. Once again, I learned that I don't know everything. This had been a recurring problem in my career. I think I'm finally over it now. I know for certain that you really never know it all. In fact, it's pretty arrogant to even think it's possible. So always listen well, and you will keep learning new things that will make you an even better leader in all areas of your life.

In that time-management seminar, I learned:

- *That I was working far too many hours and too many weekends and nights just to get my work done*

- *How to think about priorities as opposed to trying to do everything*

- *How to get big projects done by involving others and by delegating effectively*

- *How to focus on family and friends, and how to lead one complete life as opposed to thinking in terms of separating my business life and my personal life; one life is hard enough to lead without trying to lead two*

- *The concept of scheduling the priorities in your life*

That last item is why I started to schedule dinner out with Priscilla every Friday night. I was tired when I got home, but going out together and talking about the week, and finding out how Daniel was doing, and just having a quiet evening together, made all the difference in the world for our relationship. We often just went to a small inn nearby and had a hamburger and some wine. From time to time, we'd go to a fancy place, but the inn, I think, was really our favorite. It was casual, quiet, and close to home. Plus, after a while, we were regulars. When you're a regular, the whole experience gets better and better. The lesson here is: *If you treat all your customers as regulars, they might very well become regulars.*

Scheduling the priorities in your life is important. This is why I have all my daily workouts scheduled and entered into my calendar. Before I started scheduling them, I would not always get a regular workout in. When I entered them as appointments in my calendar, I made real progress. I wanted to get to retirement and beyond still alive, and, of course, staying fit is one-third of the formula. Eating right is another third, and getting enough sleep is the other. Do not even think about smoking or being around people who smoke!

I would be really angry if I'd paid all that money into Social Security for forty to fifty years and never got to collect any of it. At the least, you should set a goal of getting to retirement alive. Right now, I'm collecting my Social Security and plan to do so for a long, long time.

I learned a lot of other things in that time-management seminar too. If you want to learn everything that I did, pick up my book, *Time Management Magic: How to Get More Done Every Day and Move from Surviving to Thriving*. Learning to manage your life is vital unless you enjoy having your life be a total mess. This system will keep your life under control, and that's ultimately what time management is all about. Spend the time planning the life you want or spend a lot of time later leading a life you *don't* want.

Another thing happened to me in this period of my career. I learned about a seminar on service that was being taught at the University of Kentucky. I signed up. The two-day seminar was called "Service America!" and was taught by the author of a book by the same name, Karl Albrecht.

The guts of the seminar dealt with how to manage a service business the way manufacturing companies manage quality control on an assembly line. The seminar put to rest a common theory at that time: that service businesses were hit-and-miss with how good the service could really be on a consistent basis.

The seminar taught that you don't have to depend on luck to offer good service. Service businesses have key points of contact and services that are more critical than others, such as employee selection, training, and auditing. You can read the book if you're interested in learning more about this approach to managing a service business.

The seminar got me very excited about how we could improve service consistency with the right processes, expectations, education, and enforcement. That seminar and the time-management seminar were defining moments in altering my management style and my approach to both my business and personal responsibilities. They led directly to my deep interest in leadership. I started to read and study everything I could get my hands on about the subject.

Two other books that made an impact on me were *The One-Minute Manager* by Ken Blanchard and *7 Habits of Highly Effective People* by Stephen Covey. I still read a lot, and as I write this I'm about to start reading *From Zero to One* by Peter Thiel and Blake Masters.

I started to see leadership triumphs and failures in every story in the newspapers and weekly magazines. These lessons jumped out of the television and off the pages of the paper like they never had before. I really wanted to understand more about the impact one individual could have in causing the right things to happen. The *Service America!* book and seminar taught me one thing that has really stuck with me all of these years. I use the concept every day to get work done and to think about how we are doing.

"The Moment of Truth" is defined as the moment when the guests, customers, patients, students, passengers, etc. come into contact with a company's product or people. What happens at that moment is the name of the game. It is where expectation and reality meet. The guests or customers come with a level of expectation that has been formed in their minds by marketing and advertising campaigns, word of mouth, sales pitches, or past visits. Even they themselves develop their own expectations, by growing their anticipation in their own minds to a level far beyond what even we might have in mind for their experience.

Marketing's job is to create the expectation, and it is our job in operations to execute it so well that we meet or exceed that expectation. When operations exceeds the customer's expectation, it sets up a new expectation for their next visit. That means, at a minimum, we have to perform consistently and, ideally, always improve.

I started teaching about moments of truth, time management, and leadership, and I quickly learned that when you teach, you learn. Teaching puts you on the spot to perform better. You cannot stand up and teach and then not walk the talk. I learned that any time I want to force myself to do something, all I have to do is get in front of a few groups and tell them what I stand for and what I plan to do. This simple concept drives me to get it done.

If leaders do not walk the talk, they soon will not be taken seriously. Worst of all, they will have no followers. Without followers and a constituency, you are a leader in name only.

It was not long before I was thought of as an expert in time management, leadership, and service management. It is interesting how you can get this kind of reputation just by focusing on a few things and learning everything you can about those subjects. I think that I have read every book on leadership and management that was ever published. I then began to teach seminars all over the world to both Marriott employees and outside groups. I learned many great lessons from those two seminars that I attended. Becoming an expert in these areas turned out even better in the long run because I went on to teach the same concepts to thousands of Disney cast members, and today I have a very successful and profitable business teaching these concepts around the world to organizations of all sizes. The two seminars even helped me become a successful author.

After I became really good at practicing the time-management system, I began teaching the seminar to help others become more organized. I was also able to improve my public speaking skills by practicing on my fellow employees, with whom I was more comfortable.

I always wonder how many people go to a seminar or a class and then never do anything with what they've learned. Many, I think. One thing that really bothers me is seeing individuals giving up on themselves way too early—not trying harder and being more persistent when attempting to attain their goals and dreams. "Never, never, never give up," as Winston Churchill said.

In the book *7 Habits of Highly Effective People* by Stephen R. Covey, one of the "7 habits" is called Sharpening the Saw. This simply means that if you want to get better performance out of yourself, then you need to sharpen your skills and knowledge, just as one sharpens a saw to get better performance out of it. Going to seminars, reading, and getting hands-on experience are all Sharpening the Saw. Are you sharp or dull? When was the last time you sharpened your saw? Remember, you can't sharpen the saw only once, unless you never plan to use it again, and if that is the case, why sharpen it in the first place? The best way to hurt yourself is by using a dull blade. A dull blade is more dangerous than a sharp one because you have to use more force.

When I visited the Marriott hotels over the next few years, I would audit them and teach a time-management, service-management, and leadership class, which helped the staff become better leaders and managers. The classes also gave them an opportunity to get to know me better on a more personal level. I was providing them with the knowledge and tools they needed to do a better job.

When you do this, you are really making a difference. Teaching is the name of the game for leaders who want to leave a legacy. Teaching comes in many forms, including educating in the classroom, walking around observing and correcting, and simply setting a good example. We all remember the great teachers in our lives. I guess that's why

Priscilla has always told me, "Lee, be careful what you say and do today. They are watching you and judging you." This goes for all of us. Role modeling is the best teacher of all, at work and at home. Just remember, your children and fellow team members are always watching and listening. They do not learn their values by what you say; they learn them by what you do.

I run into people all over the world who tell me they were in one of my time-management classes twenty years ago and how much it has helped them. One woman told me that my class saved her marriage. She was so glad that her husband had attended.

Others tell me how they changed after that seminar and that it both propelled their careers and helped them in their personal lives. I love hearing this feedback from people I've helped by teaching them something I've learned. This is where the true satisfaction of leadership comes from, for me anyway. A leader's job is to produce more leaders. A parent's job is to produce children who can become great parents— and citizens and leaders as well. I even had Daniel attend my time-management seminar with a couple of his buddies before he went off to Boston University. I told him I was only paying for four years, so he needed to be organized, attend class, sit in the front row in every class, and tell the professors they were doing a good job. When the professor knows you and knows you appreciate them, they may give you a small benefit of the doubt and raise your grade. This is how real life works. People can't help you if they don't know you. Do not sit in the back.

I held the position of regional director of food and beverage at Marriott from 1979 to 1984. I opened more than 100 hotels during that period, and my life was travel, travel, and more travel. Much of my time was spent recruiting new people into the company because we were growing by leaps and bounds. You really learn how important talent is at a time like that. I so wish that I had known then about using structured interviews. I learned about them years later, at Disney, from Jan Miller of the Gallup organization, and also from my partner Carol Quinn. Carol's website is www.HireAuthority.com. Go there if you're interested in becoming an expert in interviewing and hiring. Mention my name, and she might even give you a better deal. At the very least, study her book, *Don't Hire Anyone Without Me!*

Structured interviews help you understand how people think, which is what you want to know before you hire them. Structured interviews taught me how to ask the right questions and what to listen for in the candidate's answers. When I was using only the normal interview process, I hired a lot of wrong-fit talent. I asked far too many questions that could be answered with a yes or a no. And at Marriott we were opening a hotel every two weeks, so I was hiring just about anyone I spoke to. Since then, I have learned how to hire right-fit talent, and I stopped making major errors.

I Become a Veep

In 1984, I was promoted to area vice president of hotel food and beverage. My responsibilities included half of all the Marriott hotels and resorts in the United States. The title of vice president was a perk that came with an increase in salary. Another really good perk was the great lessons I learned from the new experiences I was having. The anti-perk? Once again, it was travel, travel, and more travel. At least in those days flying was tolerable; you could get to the airport sixty seconds before your flight and not miss it. That was a mini-perk compared to traveling today.

During that time, Marriott was focused on improving its convention and catering business. Our goal was to do those things better than all the other major hotel chains. We accomplished that mission over the next few years through setting new standards for service and equipment, hiring the right people, educating (training), and enforcing. At the same time, we continued opening new hotels at a rapid pace.

Once again, I made the mistake of not taking the time to cultivate good relationships with the regional vice presidents of the different divisions of Marriott. I hit the ground running and was totally focused on getting things done, forcing changes as I saw fit, when I should have gotten the relationships right before I started with the tactics. The regional vice presidents were above me in the organization's structure, and they had a lot of influence. I realized that later than I should have, after the damage had been done. I wasn't doing anything wrong, but whether we like it or not, one cannot ignore the political angle in life. It's just the way it is, and it's never going to change. People above you can hurt your career even if they themselves are incompetent.

You put a lot of ambitious, smart individuals together, and the competition quickly begins. Sometimes it's in small, hard-to-notice ways, and sometimes it's in big, destructive ways. Often, I believe, people don't even realize how different their behavior is at work compared to in their personal lives with their family and friends. As someone once said, "You need a healthy ego to be successful, but you need to learn to check it at the door." There is a big difference between a healthy ego and being egotistical.

Relationships matter. Never forget this. You may be an outstanding performer, technically competent, and a great manager, but if you don't have strong political and relational skills, you risk failure or, at a minimum, disappointment. Leaders who have good one-on-one relationships and good multi-relationships are simply more successful and able to get more things accomplished. This is not rocket science, but many people find it extremely difficult to live by. Go for the win-win when you can, not just the win for you at any cost. As they say, "Save your bullets for the really big battles."

This phenomenon happens at every level. There are perfectly normal, nice people who become weird when they get to work. A lot of it has to do with insecurity and greed. It also has to do with unhealthy egos that make people egotistical and self-centered. And, of course, a lot of it has to do with selfish ambition, as well as many other factors. It's a sad thing, and those who behave that way rarely figure out that people are laughing at them and talking about them behind their backs. I worked with very senior people like that at Hilton, Marriott, and Disney, and I run into them frequently in my own business today. At my leadership seminars, I often hear this: "My boss needs your seminar badly." There's a big difference between what you do, how much money you make, and who you really are.

Make sure you have the same leadership style and behavior both up and down the chain of command. If you don't, people will see it and you will lose credibility. Have you ever seen leaders who are totally different in front of their boss compared to how they are with their direct reports? The people who report to you see the real you; make sure that's the way your boss sees you as well.

I made many mistakes early in my career because I did not understand the importance of good relationship skills. Did that make me a fool? Yes, it did! I've since become much better in this area, and now I'm "me" twenty-four hours a day . . . for better or worse. It's much too hard to have different personalities, especially when your boss and your direct reports are in the same room.

The bottom line is: if people don't not like you or trust you, then you won't get very far, and you may never quite know why because no one will tell you. It really is common sense; but as we know, common sense is less and less common. Even if you attain a big, prestigious position, if people don't respect you, it might not be worth it. All you have is your own reputation in life. I'm not the same person I was when I started out in business. I realized that I wanted my family, friends, and colleagues to remember me as a good man rather than a selfish, attain-success-at-any-cost nut. If I'd kept on going the way I was headed in my early days, I would be the only one at my funeral one day.

The Veep Goes Global

In November 1985, I was promoted to vice president of food and beverage planning for all Marriott hotels and resorts around the world. That was a very interesting job because I got to plan the hotel food and beverage operations from the ground up. Plus, I got to travel all over the world, learning valuable lessons in Hong Kong, Mexico, Poland, and many other places. When you travel, you really grow in knowledge and wisdom.

In Hong Kong I learned just how great service could be. The service I experienced there was like nowhere else I'd ever been. That's why I came to believe you cannot provide service that is better than what you've experienced yourself. It's critical to get out and about and experience the world so you know what's possible. Knowing what's possible can drive you to achieve higher and higher levels of excellence. See the world; touch it, hear it, smell it, and taste it! Direct experience is far different from reading about things or watching programs about them on TV or YouTube.

I was so impressed with the service in Asia that Priscilla and I took Daniel there to add to his education when he graduated from high school in 1987. We spent a month in Japan, Hong Kong, and China, and the trip left us with lasting impressions that I know influenced the way we think today. That's what travel and new experiences do. They change you.

They open your eyes and mind to the possibilities in life. People often ask me what one thing contributed the most to my success. The answer? I got out of the little town I grew up in and experienced what was happening in the rest of the world. So far, I've visited forty-nine countries and had both unbelievable and valuable experiences in every single one of them. Travel is the very best way to overcome bigotry as well.

I went to Mexico once to research two hotel projects for Marriott. The man who picked me up in Puerto Vallarta did not speak one word of English, and I knew about three words in Spanish. Somehow, we managed to communicate. In our three days together we got all our work done and had a great time to boot. The bonding started when we showed one another pictures of our sons. We had in common that we were both proud fathers. The lesson: *There is always common ground. You just have to look for it.*

Another memorable experience was when I worked on a Marriott hotel project in Warsaw, Poland. This was before the Berlin Wall came down. When I landed in Warsaw, there were police with automatic weapons everywhere, and when I met with the local people on the construction project, a Communist Party member was always present to listen to the conversations. If you have not experienced such a thing, I can assure you it leaves a lasting impression about the wonderful freedoms we have in America.

At our first meeting in Warsaw, I was offered vodka at 9:00 a.m. I said, "No, thanks." My host was surprised. "You don't drink?" he said. In those days, I was not drinking any alcohol, so I said no and ordered a cup of coffee. "Never?" the man said. I believe that for the rest of the trip he thought there was something seriously wrong with me. By the way, I love wine now, but I stop drinking alcoholic beverages for a few weeks several times a year just to make sure I can. This is called self-discipline.

Before leaving Poland, having completed my research on possible concepts for the Warsaw Marriott, I had a final meeting with the local team. I told them I was going to create an all-day dining café, and it would be named after a famous Polish poet. They liked that. I told them we would also have a grill room concept for steaks and chops and similar dishes. I asked them if we could name it the American Grill.

The Communist Party member just about had a heart attack. "No, no!" he said excitedly. "You cannot use words that have America in them."

"Okay," I said, "What about California Grill?"

He said, "No, that is too close to Reagan."

At that time, Ronald Reagan was the president of the United States, and since he was from California that was considered the wrong name for the restaurant. Then I thought of a better choice. I had lived in Chicago at two different times, and I knew that Chicago had more Polish immigrants than any city in the world. "What about Chicago Grill?" I said.

A big smile came over the party member's face. "Yes. Chicago good. Many Polish people in Chicago." That's how the Chicago Grill at the Warsaw Marriott was born.

I learned a lot about diversity and inclusiveness as I traveled the world doing my job. When you travel and get to know the people, you find out that they're the same everywhere. They're just trying to have a decent life. They're trying to make things better for their children. They're proud of their families, their religion, their culture, and their country.

I spent a lot of time in libraries doing research on food concepts for places all over the world when the Internet was in its infancy and there were no search engines like Google. I still like to go to the library for a few hours to work. Wherever I am, the library is a great place to think and dream. No one bothers you there, and the librarians are knowledgeable and helpful. On business trips today, when I want a quiet place to work, I go to the public library. You can even use their computers if you don't want to drag yours along.

Another Roller Coaster Plunge

One day I learned that my boss, Karl Kilburg, senior vice president of food and beverage, was going to become a vice president in charge of a region of Marriott hotels. Karl's current position was one I was always sure I'd get one day. I was more than qualified for it, and I could think of no reason why I would not be promoted when the job became open.

Well, subtle hints started to come, telling me I would probably not get it. Everyone danced around it for months until one day Karl finally told me the truth. I would not get the job because some of the regional vice presidents did not support me. They remembered the years I ran roughshod over them to get things done. By the way, that was the very first time I'd heard such a comment. I'd always had top annual ratings, and no one had ever discussed those issues with me. Lesson: *Don't count on people telling you the truth. Don't be naïve.*

Five regional vice presidents supported me, and four did not. I happened to see the list on Karl's desk, and I could read upside down very well. There was a yes or no next to each name. I spent the next few months fixing my relationship problems with the four who did not support me. Since I wasn't getting the big job, I told Karl I wanted to leave Marriott headquarters and be general manager of one of the hotels. There was no way I could stay where I was and work for anyone else.

I can tell you that during that time, I was not a happy camper. I started going home early and putting less effort into my work. I was very disappointed and angry about not getting the job. I was probably suffering from mild depression too. My last disappointment had been fifteen years earlier when I was fired. I'd had a run of fifteen years of one promotion after another, and success after success. Remember that career roller coaster I told you about? I was about to get another ride on the "Big-Drop Career Coaster," which is unsettling to your stomach and makes Rock 'n' Roller Coaster at Disney look like child's play.

At first, my request for a general manager position was answered with a no, and by now you know that I do not like the word *no* very much. They said I would have to be a resident manager first. I went professionally ballistic, and soon I was offered a general manager's job—in the smallest hotel in the company. The hotel, in Springfield, Massachusetts, was not only small but it was old, and it hadn't been renovated in years.

I accepted the job. I'm sure they thought I would quit, but I didn't. By then, I had been in the hotel business for twenty-three years but I'd never managed a hotel. I thought taking a step down was a good idea because it would give me more opportunities in the future. At the moment, things did not look great for my career, but that trusty roller coaster soon started back up, and the ride turned out to be more exciting than I could ever have imagined. Little did I know that coaster would take me to a Magic Kingdom and The Walt Disney Company.

At this point in my story I was forty-four years old. Daniel was nineteen and in his first year at Boston University. I'd been married for twenty years, and Priscilla and I were about to make our ninth move. One reason the previous assignment had been good was that Daniel started fourth grade in Rockville, Maryland, and went all the way to college without our relocating during that period. It was a major perk for our family.

I had earned many millions in experience during those eight years. I had achieved several promotions. I had been a vice president for four years, and now I was going to learn how to manage a hotel. We even had some money in the bank and investments in the stock market.

In chapter 6, I'll tell you about my adventures as general manager of a hotel and why the move turned out to be one of the most important of my career.

Insights

Moving and adapting is the best education.

Children adapt quickly.

Perks and anti-perks are real.

Lead with respect, influence, and expertise.

Learn to be a partner.

Learn from role models.

You get what you reward.

Know when to change your approach.

Recessions come and go.

Learn from children.

Be careful what you say and do.

Don't forget about your loved ones.

A time-management course can change your life and accelerate your career.

International travel changes you for the better.

You might be passed over or fired, but your future can still include pixie dust and a bright wish-upon-a-star future.

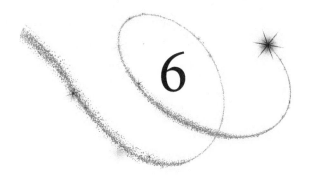

General Manager: 1988–1990

It was 1988, and I'd been working in the hotel business for twenty-three years. All twenty-three were in food and beverage. I started as a banquet server, and I rose to the level of vice president. I was sure that my next promotion would be to senior vice president of food and beverage for the Marriott corporation, but, as I previously mentioned, it was not to be. My career was starting to feel like a pogo stick. So I thought long and hard about my situation and decided that the best thing for my future would be to become general manager of a hotel. I successfully negotiated a deal with one of the regional vice presidents.

Frankly, we never thought we would leave the Washington area. We loved our home, our neighborhood, and our friends. We had family in the area as well. In fact, things seemed to be quite perfect until the blip in my career that led us to Springfield, Massachusetts, and Marriott's smallest hotel. It had been another brand of hotel until Marriott took it over a few years prior. Old and run down, with only 250 rooms, it was owned by the Massachusetts Mutual Life Insurance Company, which had its headquarters in Springfield. (Marriott does not own most of its hotels; it manages them on a management contract for the owners.)

Priscilla and I went to Springfield one weekend to take a look at it. When we walked into the hotel, Priscilla said, "Lee, what did you do to deserve this place? What did you do to those people back at headquarters?"

All we could do was laugh. The alternative was to cry! Do not assume that someone who's laughing is happy.

When we got back to Washington, my boss, Karl Kilburg, held a nice going-away party for me and said many kind things about me. You know how it goes. When you're leaving, everyone loves you. "Lee is great and one of our best leaders," Karl said. "He is personally responsible for much of our success over the last few years."

I was thinking, *And that is why they gave me the Springfield Marriott*? I didn't say it, and neither did Karl. I gave a very professional thank-you speech. I said I was very excited to have the opportunity and really appreciated all the support I was receiving blah, blah, blah . . . at least by then I had learned how not to burn bridges the way I had earlier in my career.

By the way, I do believe that I've been at least 51 percent responsible for the various difficulties I experienced in my career. I don't blame it all on others, and while I could say that I often did not receive the feedback I needed, or help on my leadership behavior, there are some things in life that you need to figure out yourself. We're in an age when it seems as though everyone wants to blame someone else for his or her circumstances, or sue someone for something. However, much of the time we're responsible for the situations we find ourselves in.

People want to blame the government, the weather, their boss, partner, wife, husband, mother, father, sister, genetic makeup, and on and on. No one seems to want to blame himself or herself, which is where most of the blame really lies.

Priscilla and I decided that I would go ahead to Springfield first; she would visit on weekends and move in about three months. She had a lot of things to take care of, and she was working for a friend who needed her. Dan and Pat Pewett were among our best and most trusted friends in Washington. Pat passed away from cancer several years ago, but we still make sure we see Dan and spend time with him a couple of times a year.

One thing I seem to be really good at is not being in town on moving day. Priscilla says I do it on purpose. We moved a lot, and I somehow always seemed to have an important meeting on moving day. "It's not my fault," I always told her with a grin.

It worked out perfectly because I moved into the Springfield Marriott hotel and lived there for three months.

When you live, eat, and sleep in the hotel you work in, you learn a lot very quickly; actually, you learn things you would never learn if you didn't live there. I learned that at 5:00 a.m. it took ten minutes for hot water to arrive at the fourteenth floor, where my room was. I kept a hot water time log each day because the director of engineering didn't believe me. I finally convinced him by personally climbing into the ceiling and finding a closed valve on a recirculation line. I wondered how long that problem had been going on, how many guests had suffered because of it, and how much compensation we had given out. It turned out to be the beginning of the end for the director of engineering. Where there's smoke, there's fire.

In my Day-Timer planner, I wrote down everything I could think of that I wanted to know about the hotel. Every day for the first month, I would meet with my department heads and ask them the questions I'd written down. If they knew the answer, they told me. If they didn't, they told me the next day or as soon as they could find out what we needed to know. I told them, "It's okay to not know the answers, but please do not make the answers up."

A number of years earlier, I'd received this advice: When you arrive at a new position, take the time during your first thirty days to write down everything that seems like it's wrong or needs improving, and then spend your time there fixing those issues. After the first month or two, you will no longer see things the same way you did when you first got there. It was great advice. I wanted to know things like:

- *How much is our maintenance budget?*

- *What are the electric costs each year?*

- *What are the water costs each year?*

- *How many people work in each department, and what are their responsibilities?*

- *What are the food costs?*

- *What was the hotel's profit the previous year?*

- *What are our costs involving employee accidents? What is our accident frequency?*

The process got me up to speed very quickly, and it made me more observant while dealing with issues and going around the property each day.

I personally approved and signed off on all the invoices for all departments so I could become familiar with what we were buying and what we were spending on every single item. This is a very productive and informative thing to do. If you control the spending, you control the profit. Things as simple as the price of tomatoes can make a big difference. During the 1980s, when McDonald's introduced a burger with tomatoes on it, tomato prices went through the roof for a while. (You learn these things from reading the paper every morning, by the way.) I asked the chef to remove the tomatoes from salads until they came down in price.

When I saw the cost of certain outside services, I told my engineer to stop using them. I had him work up a reduced-cost solution. You'll be amazed by what triggers your mind when you see the cost and quantities of the things you're buying. Review every single invoice in your business, and you will be amazed at what you learn.

In the first week, I went around asking each department head which one thing he or she most wanted for their department.

- *Housekeeping told me they wanted a new carpet in the lobby, as the one there was embarrassing.*

- *The banquet staff said they needed more hangers for the coatroom. I immediately told one of them to go to a store and buy them, and to bring me the receipt.*

- *The restaurant team told me they needed more silverware, and also more fresh fish on the menu. We ordered the flatware that day and started two fresh fish specials the following Monday.*

- *The owners of the hotel, MassMutual, told me they hated the plastic flowers above the revolving door in the lobby. I had them removed that night.*

I did something similar for every single department. I wanted each one to show immediate improvement when I provided them with what they needed to do their jobs. Putting that new carpet in the lobby made me famous with the staff. You would have thought I'd renovated the entire hotel.

When a department head asked for something really big or too expensive, I got back to them with an answer about when we might be able to do it, or I told them the reason why we would not be able to. Telling people why is really important. I gained a lot of credibility and quick wins with the staff that way. At that point in my career, I had learned to ask questions, listen more, talk less, and take quick action.

I joined the Springfield Convention and Visitors Bureau. I went to the Rotary Club meeting every Friday. I joined the board of the Chamber of Commerce. I established excellent relationships with the mayor, the local congressman, and the owners, MassMutual. Our hotel was downtown, so these relationships were important. I had never been involved much in a community before, so there were lots of good learning opportunities for me. In a small community, you cannot hide! You have to participate and be involved. Get involved with your community!

The community expected both Priscilla and me to be involved, and we were. Priscilla started teaching in a literacy program. She would make me hire her students as soon as she taught them to read. "A job builds self-confidence and self-esteem," she would tell me, and she kept the pressure on me to find a place for people who had the drive to get ahead.

One of her students was a woman who had never traveled far from home because she literally could not find her way back. She could speak English and Spanish but could not read in either language. One day her kids asked her to make cookies and she couldn't read the recipe. She also wanted to be able to read them a story before they went to sleep. That's when she signed up for Priscilla's class. She went on to get her driver's license and a job, and her life improved dramatically.

The satisfaction one gets from teaching someone to read is enormous. Priscilla even received an award from the governor for her work.

My office was initially located on the fourth floor of the hotel, in the back of the sales and marketing area. I immediately had an office built for me behind the front desk in the lobby, with a door that led right to the reception desk. I told the front desk staff to come and get me any time they needed me to handle a guest situation, because I never wanted them to become rude. I left the door that led from my office to the check-in desk open most of the time so they knew I meant it . . . and so I could hear how they were speaking to our guests.

I had a counter built at the end of the front desk so that twenty-four hours a day guests could buy miscellaneous items they needed, such as aspirin, a shirt, a tie, magazines, or a newspaper. During all the years I spent traveling, I hated seeing a hotel shop closed when I needed something. The front desk team looked after the area. Although this is common in hotels today, it was not back then.

I had a resident manager (the number two position in a hotel) named Doreen Robinson. She worked days just as I did, so a lot of issues and problems came up on the night shift. Since most guests arrived from 4:00 p.m. on, I needed mature, experienced leadership at night. In a business hotel, not too many problems occur between 9:00 a.m. and 5:00 p.m. because the guests check out between 7:00 a.m. and 9:00 a.m. and arrive between 4:00 p.m. and 8:00 p.m. For that reason, I always made sure to have the right leadership on duty at the right times. Ultimately, this was the reason I arrived at 6:00 a.m., before my guests woke up.

I told Doreen she had to begin working from 3:00 p.m. to 1:00 a.m. I would be the day general manager, and she would be the evening general manager. I'm not sure she appreciated my humor on the subject. She had worked daytime hours for her entire career, so she was probably unhappy about the change. But she agreed to it, and she did the job so well that my problems at night went away immediately. She was a real professional.

Chief Inspector

My schedule was very routine. I believe in routine because it produces consistency and builds accountability in operations. That said, I must admit that routine can also be very boring. Peter Drucker, the management guru of the twentieth century, once said, "Management is boring. If you want excitement, become a race car driver."

I arrived every day at 6:00 a.m. I first checked the driveway, lobby, and all three public elevators for cleanliness. You would be surprised what you will find in elevators or in a driveway in the morning. They're usually things you do not want your guests to see. I even checked the blue USPS mailbox on the corner to make sure it was clean. Mr. Marriott had once told me to keep mailboxes clean if they are near the hotel.

I then took an elevator up to the fourteenth floor and walked every floor in the hotel to make sure there were no room-service trays or tables in the hallways with nasty-looking dirty dishes from the night before (I hate that). Have you ever seen a piece of prime rib on a plate in a hotel hallway twelve hours after it was served to the guest? It's not a pretty sight. I also wanted to make sure that the express checkouts and newspapers had been delivered, and that the floors and stairwells were clean.

When I first started doing all that, I would find a lot of trays in the halls. After I explained my expectations to my room-service team in that area, it wasn't long before I did not see another one. Everyone knew I checked every morning without fail. I think they checked the halls at midnight, and again around fifteen minutes before I got there. It's amazing how being a good role model and setting high expectations gets things done, especially if you personally check up on your expectations. As some experts say, "Inspect what you expect."

I worked my way down to the fourth floor, arriving there around 6:15. That was the floor where all the banquet, convention space, and production kitchens were. I walked the whole area while the banquet team was setting up for breakfast and meetings. I walked the front and then the back to see if everything had been put away and locked up the night before. I checked every storeroom and kitchen to see if we were in good shape and ready for breakfast. I looked in every walk-in cooler to make sure the food was dated and rotated properly and that the third shift had left the place spotless. As I made my daily tours through all departments, I noted safety issues and asked the staff if they knew of any. I also thanked them for doing a great job and told them I would see them again later that day.

I then checked the employee cafeteria and the employee locker rooms for cleanliness. I wanted the locker rooms to look great so when employees arrived at work they had clean, well-maintained rooms to get ready in. I wanted the showers, locker room, and toilets clean enough that I would want to use them. Back when I was a frontline employee, the facilities were often disgusting. Once I rose to more senior positions, I had the authority to fix things like that. I checked every single public restroom as well, including the ladies', because not many guests were around that early.

After that, I worked my way down to the lobby level and checked the driveway and the lobby conditions again, as our guests would soon be coming down for breakfast and checkout. As I said, guests leave early in a business hotel, so people in various positions require different schedules.

I would then head to the restaurant to make sure the breakfast setup was going well. By then, it would be 6:45. I would check out room service and head down to the basement to check the receiving dock and the trash dumpster for cleanliness and security. I would then check in with the morning maintenance team to see if there were any issues to deal with. By 7:00, I would make my way to my office with a full Day-Timer of notes to review with my executive committee. They knew that in twenty-four hours I would be taking my walk again, so they needed to get their assignments accomplished and fix any problems before then. Safety issues were always to be fixed first and immediately.

From 7:00 to 8:30 a.m., I walked the banquet spaces again, greeting every meeting planner and assisting them with any last-minute needs they had. I checked the restaurants several times and hung out in the lobby to talk with guests and help the staff with any difficult issues that might arise. I would schedule no meetings before 9:00 a.m. because I wanted to be out and about with my staff and guests.

I made the tour again from 11:00 a.m. to noon. I went to the health club and worked out from 3:00 to 4:00 p.m. I inspected rooms from 4:00 to 5:00, and then again between 5:00 and 6:00. I did my routine evening tour, and then I was out of there. I was home at 6:10 p.m., unless there was an important evening event in the hotel, in which case I'd go home and return for the event. Living close to work made this possible.

With this routine, I got to see every employee every day on all three shifts. Everyone knew who I was and what I wanted. The third-shift cleaner told me he had been there for ten years and I was the first general manager he'd ever actually met and, for that matter, had ever even *seen*.

I implemented checklist systems in every department and checked them for compliance as I walked around. I also used these walks to show employees the right way to do a task, from something as small as how to cut lemon wedges properly to how to use a knife safely; from how to lift heavy objects to how to respond better the next time in a guest situation.

I had a desk and telephone installed in the lobby right in front of the check-in desk and had a nameplate made that said Lee Cockerell, General Manager. I would sit out there and do my work several hours a day so guests could talk with me and the staff could see me and send guests over as well. That really blew them away. You do some things for effect. My staff knew I was serious about excellence.

And I personally created our mission statement. I did not ask anyone's opinion or set up a committee to study it. I made it simple so no one would forget it: "Be so nice to the guests that they can't believe it." I believe that simple sentence was the number one takeaway from the Springfield chapter in my life. Do that and you will be rewarded with great business results.

I told all my employees that if they would do that one thing, I would provide them with whatever resources and training they needed to get their jobs done. I still get notes from some of them that end with "Lee, don't forget to be so nice to the guests that they can't believe it." Even now, if you go to that hotel in Springfield, you will find employees who remember this and practice it. Being nice is the most important service standard you can have, as my then thirteen-year-old granddaughter, Margot, told me when I was writing my second book, *The Customer Rules: The 39 Essential Rules for Delivering Sensational Service.*

Every afternoon from 4:00 to 5:00 p.m., I did what I called a one-minute inspection of thirty rooms. This entailed walking into the room and seeing how it felt, looked, and smelled. I wore a little apron with pockets where I kept extra bars of soap, shampoo, and a rag.

If a bar of soap was missing, I replaced it; if the mirror had a spot on it, I wiped it. I made a note of such things in my Day-Timer, and when I was finished, I discussed it with the housekeeper who had cleaned that room and later with the executive housekeeper. That way, I got a look at every room in the hotel every eight or nine days. I told the housekeepers that one major thing I needed from them was no hair in the bathrooms. Hair in a bathroom, especially when it is not yours, is a major problem. They thought that was funny, but they remembered it. Every time I saw a housekeeper, I would say, "No hair." After a while, when they saw me, they would say, "No hair," even if they did not speak English. I told them I could handle a little dust on the picture frames, but no hair in the bathrooms!

Experience Pays Dividends

The reason I was able to be a great general manager, even though I had never done it before, was that I had traveled constantly for almost ten years. I had checked into and out of more hotel rooms than I want to think about. I had stayed in and used the services of the best hotels in the world. I knew what was important from a guest's perspective, and that is what I focused on. That's why no hair in the bathroom was at the top of my list.

I placed a full-size ironing board and an iron in every room because ironing on one of those miniature boards is ridiculous, and waiting for them to be delivered is painful. This amenity is pretty common today but was not back then.

I put a note on the dresser of every room. It said, "If you need anything or if anything is wrong, let me know," and was signed Lee Cockerell, General Manager. Similarly, I put a round gold sticker on all the restaurant menus that said, "If you have any problems that the restaurant manager cannot or will not resolve, call me twenty-four hours a day. The operator and the restaurant manager have my home phone number."

Believe it or not, I never received a call. I wonder why. The day those stickers went on the menus, service in the restaurant immediately improved.

Here are some of the other things I did:

- *I opened the health club/exercise room twenty-four hours a day because my travels had taught me that many people need to get in there early or late. This is common today, but it wasn't back then.*

- *I built that miscellaneous counter into the end of the desk so guests could get the things they needed twenty-four hours a day. That too is common today but was not back then.*

- *I put an express breakfast buffet in place to speed up service, as business guests are always in a hurry.*

- *I put coffee and coffee makers in the rooms because it's one of the most important things to business travelers, especially first thing in the morning. This is also common today but was not back then.*

I got really focused on the safety issue when my bonus was hit hard the first year I was there because of high accident frequency. We started a stretching program for all the housekeepers every morning to cut down on back strains. We made it a policy that housekeepers were not allowed to turn a mattress alone. We made sure they wore eye protection when they sprayed chemicals. And I put up signs in all the back-of-the-house areas that read: "SAFETY:

If a safety issue exists that your manager is not fixing, or if you have any concerns about a safe work environment that your manager is not addressing, call me twenty-four hours a day. The operator has my home phone number and will get me on the line. Lee Cockerell, General Manager, Extension 5434."

Again, I never got a call. The managers learned to take care of these things and to pay attention to employee concerns, ideas, and suggestions. I put in place high expectations and total accountability.

In food and beverage, I had a good heart-to-heart talk with my executive chef and told him that the kitchen floors must always be dry and he needed to figure out how to make that happen. Also, all food-preparation employees were required to wear protective gloves when using knives. I went through every department and put procedures and safety rules in place. As a result, our accident frequency plummeted.

- *If the floors are dry, you do not fall.*

- *If you have a glove on (including management to set a good example), you do not get cuts.*

- *If you stretch, you have fewer back injuries, and so on.*

Everyone who had an accident had to come see me with his or her manager and explain what had happened. What was written on the accident report was often quite different from what the employee had described to me. I was looking for the real causes so I could institute operating guidelines and training to prevent the same thing from happening again. I couldn't do that if I didn't know the real reason an accident happened.

I interrogated the employee the way Judge Judy does to learn the truth. If someone was out of work with a lost-time accident, we visited him or her at home and kept closely in touch so everyone knew we cared, we missed them, and we wanted to see them back at work. I personally called each injured employee frequently at home to see how he or she was coming along.

The hotel was so small that I was able to be everywhere. One thing I learned for sure is that what is important to the general manager of a hotel is what is important to the staff. I guarantee you that the general manager is the most important person in any organization; the corporate folks are not.

Team Play

The Springfield position turned out to be the best job I'd had up to that point in my career. I was able to make a difference every day for my guests and staff. I would not have been able to do that in a bureaucratic headquarters office.

I set up an advisory group of frontline employees from every department and met with them every Thursday for an hour. In addition, I had my director of human resources and director of maintenance in the room, as most of the problems that employees brought up related to those two areas.

My secretary, Angie Rowe, took down everything the employees told me, from a leaky faucet that needed repairing to equipment shortages; from safety issues to a broken vacuum cleaner. We sent the list to the department heads every week so they could fix the problems, ideally before the next Thursday. Angie was very organized and followed up on everything for me. The lesson? If you have a secretary or an administrative assistant, make sure they are highly organized, with strong administrative skills.

The following Thursday, we went over each task on the list to see if it had been completed. Every item was chronologically numbered, and it stayed on the list until it was resolved. We posted that list on all the bulletin boards so employees could see that I was listening to them and getting things accomplished. I was removing the hassles from their jobs so they could perform at the highest level, and in turn remove hassles for our guests.

This is the power of routine and process. The more issues I took care of, the more my associates told me about. I learned to build high trust by involving the staff in their work. This process made sure that nothing was forgotten or slipped through the cracks.

If someone brings something to your attention and you do not follow up, your credibility falls to zero. It's easy to believe that an issue is too small and too unimportant to follow up on. What I learned, however, was that while it may be a small issue to me, it was often a crucial issue for the person bringing it to my attention. I wanted to have 100 percent credibility with 100 percent of our staff.

I learned that it's important to make sure your associates know exactly what you do for them. Whenever I did something to improve my team's working conditions, I let them know what I had done.

One day, the first week I was in Springfield, I walked into the grand ballroom just before a luncheon for three hundred guests was to begin. I noticed a cigarette burn in the tablecloth on one of the banquet tables. I told Sharon, the banquet captain, to change the tablecloth.

She looked at me like I was crazy. The doors were going to open in a few minutes. She said, "I'll just put the salt and pepper shakers over the burn hole."

I said, "No. Change it."

"But we are about to open the doors," she protested.

"Then you'd better hurry," I told her.

She did not realize that I knew a lot about the banquet department, as that's where I got my start. I think she thought I was a nut. Ten years later, when I was working at Disney, I received a letter from Sharon. I had of course long forgotten the cigarette burn incident. She said she wanted to thank me for setting such an example of excellence and attention to detail back in Springfield. She recounted the story and said that encounter with me had changed the way she thought about her management responsibilities as well as her personal and professional standards. She said it was the main reason she had become so successful.

Never forget that if you are going to be excellent, everything matters. Attention to detail is the name of the game for excellence in all things. All leaders are molded by their experiences in life and the people they work for and with. Never underestimate the impact you can have on someone. That's what happened between Sharon and me that morning.

Boy, I love to hear stories like that. As a leader, influencing people for the better is where the big satisfaction and payoff come. It's like your grown children telling you how much they appreciate the way you raised them, even though there were moments along the way when they did not care much for your parental direction.

One thing I always did was to make sure frontline employees knew that leadership was available when they needed us. For example, if a situation with a guest became too difficult to handle, they were to remain polite and professional and then get a leader to help out, even if that leader was in a meeting at the time. The guests came first. And supporting the frontline cast was a close second. My policy was that if a guest had an issue and asked to see the manager, we would not tell the guest that the manager was unavailable because he or she was in a meeting. There is seldom, if ever, a meeting more important than a customer.

During a major renovation of the hotel in Springfield, we had to close the lobby for months and have our guests check in on the banquet level on the fourth floor. The restaurants would also be closed, and temporary restaurants would be set up in banquet rooms. I anticipated having some unhappy guests during that time. Knowing this, I did not want my front desk staff to get so worked over by the guests day after day that they'd become rude and unprofessional. So I made sure we had a table set up next to the temporary front desk. A manager was stationed there from 6:00 to 9:00 a.m. and again from 4:00 to 8:00 p.m. to handle difficult guest issues on the spot. At other times, a manager would be paged. I was one of the managers who often took duty at that table.

One directive I gave was that if someone applied for a job and had previously worked for Disney, we should hire them. I knew that Disney's selection process was excellent and their training was even better. We had great success doing this; every ex-Disney employee turned out to be great. Getting a job at a well-respected organization such as Hilton, Marriott, Disney, Apple, or Google will pay off in your career.

Moving On
That general manager's position was great because it gave me an opportunity to try out all of the management and leadership concepts I had learned over the previous few years. It gave me experience working in the community, and it gave

me a chance to learn more about our guests because many of them stayed with us frequently. Most of all, though, it gave me the chance to see how great a leader I could become.

I learned the challenge of having to worry about and balance guest satisfaction, staff attitudes and performance, morale, and business results. It was quite different from being in a staff role, and much more satisfying as well.

When in July 1990 I left Springfield to join Disney, a typical management going-away party was thrown. It was a very nice event, but what really made my day was that the frontline employees took up a collection, rented the Veterans of Foreign Wars Hall in Springfield, and threw an additional party for Priscilla and me. They gave each of us a very nice plaque, engraved with lovely words about how much they appreciated our leadership, great example, and friendship. When the frontline employees do that, you know you've been a great leader for them. They spent their own money on that party. Nothing like it had ever happened to me before—and it hasn't happened since, for that matter.

Our family had gone through a lot of difficult things from 1988 to 1990. My mother was diagnosed with lung cancer and died. Four months later, so did my grandmother and idol. And while we were attending her funeral, Priscilla's dad stepped out of his car in Annapolis and was struck by another vehicle. He ended up in Bethesda Naval Hospital for months. All that, plus my brother had bypass surgery.

One thing I know for sure is that if you smoke, *stop*! My mother always said she could never stop smoking. She tried many times. Finally, the day the doctor told her she had lung cancer, she stopped. It was too late. If not for cigarettes, she might still be here today; she would have gotten to know her three great-grandchildren, and they would know her. If you won't stop for yourself, then stop for your family and friends. Do not let a little piece of paper wrapped around a plant be stronger than you are.

By June 1990, everyone in our family was either gone or recovering from various illnesses, so Priscilla and I were ready to do something new. The hotel was running beautifully. We had completed a $12 million renovation. I had a great team. The challenge was over. I was getting bored again.

Priscilla's life was looking up too. When we moved to Springfield, I was given a new company car, so I bought my old company car and gave it to Priscilla. It was the newest car she had ever owned, and it was three years old. After driving VW Bugs for years, and the old lemon of a Chrysler that her dad had given her, she was pretty happy with that car. She considered it brand new.

My career roller coaster was moving and grooving. I had been working for twenty-five years and was completing my nineteenth job. I was forty-five years old. Priscilla and I were a little nervous, but we were very happy and excited about our next adventure. We had been married for twenty-two years and were about to relocate for the ninth time. Daniel was in his third year at Boston University. I figured I had accumulated $7 million in experience, and it was starting to pay off. Experience, I've learned, is like money in the bank in its own unique way.

I told you that when I left Marriott corporate headquarters in 1988 as a vice president to serve as general manager at a tiny hotel in Springfield, it would turn out to be the best decision of my life. In chapter 7, I'll tell you why.

Insights

Don't burn bridges.

Be wary of exit interviews.

Your problems are at least 51 percent your fault.

Get up to speed quickly.

Ask questions, and ask, ask, ask some more.

Get involved in your community.

Routine is powerful.

Be visible.

Add high value to the guest/customer experience.

Focus on safety as you would with your children.

Returns on experience and knowledge are huge.

You are not a product of your circumstances; you are a product of your decisions.

As Seen In The Main Street Leader

There is only One Purpose

At the Walt Disney World Resort, there are hundreds of roles, but there is only ONE purpose…to make sure every Guest has the most fabulous time of their life.

The custodial teams' role is to ensure guests and cast have a clean environment to work and play in. And they know what their purpose is as well.

That is why you see them giving out guide maps in all languages to guests.

That is why you see them talking to young children and giving them character stickers.

That is what you see them giving directions and laughing with guests when they give inside hints on how to enjoy Walt Disney World.

The Custodial Team knows their purpose well, and they perform their roles (jobs) well, too.

Walt Disney World is world-famous as a clean vacation destination, thanks to the outstanding custodial team.

Does every member of your team understand their work goes beyond their assigned role? Is the work they do bigger than a job?

Once every team member knows their purpose and how their role contributes to the purpose, you will build a remarkable reputation, too.

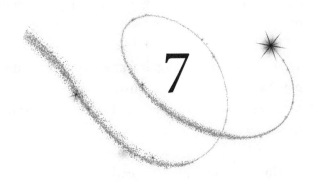

Vive la France: 1990–1993

I had learned that there was life after dropping out of college . . . life after the army . . . life after Hilton . . . life after getting fired . . . life after being passed over for an expected promotion . . . and I was about to learn there was life after Marriott.

Almost everyone survives the thrill of a ride on the Big Career Roller Coaster as long as they stay seated, keep their seatbelts fastened, stay professional, stay positive, go with the flow, and have fun! When it stops, just get off and get refocused for the next ride. The other word for this is *life*!

In June 1990, I was really enjoying life as a general manager in Springfield. I may not have been a vice president, but I was a "big deal" in the Springfield Marriott. I made 99 percent of the decisions about the hotel without checking with anyone. By contrast, when I was a vice president in Washington, D.C., I was a small fish in a big pond. Life as a big fish in a small pond was very good indeed. *What more could I want?* I sometimes asked myself.

Well, one day the phone rang. It was a Disney executive named Sanjay Varma, who was responsible for opening what was then called Euro Disney Resort and is today Disneyland Paris. I had worked with him years before at Marriott. At one point, he reported to me, and later we were peers. He had left Marriott a couple of years earlier to join Disney. Now he was calling to offer me a position at Disney in Paris, reporting to him.

This is going to happen to many people in their professional careers, so make sure you're respectful and nice to everyone on your way up. You never know who will be your boss one day. It may well be someone who reported to you at one time, and they will remember the real you. Direct reports often have a different opinion of you than your peers and your boss do.

The position Sanjay was offering was director of food and beverage and quality assurance. He told me that Euro Disney Resort was scheduled to open on April 12, 1992, which was two years away.

I was thinking, *I was in food and beverage for twenty-three years before I became a general manager. Why would I want to do this?*

I clearly understood why Sanjay wanted me to take the position. Food and beverage is what I had the most expertise in, and he needed someone who could organize the food and beverage operations. He wanted someone who was good at organizing big projects, and I was very good at that.

We had completed a $12 million renovation of the 250-room hotel in Springfield. The place looked great and was running perfectly. As a result, Marriott loved me again. I knew it would not be long before they gave me a bigger hotel to run. Plus, I was enjoying a lot of perks: great salary, company car, excellent health care plan, and stock options. I lived only eight minutes from work, and Daniel was only ninety minutes away at Boston University. We saw him frequently at his rugby games and at other times as well. Life was almost perfect.

So why in the world would I give up what most people would consider an almost-perfect life to start over with a different company in high-risk conditions? The answer is simple: I was bored, and boredom is mentally painful and will affect your performance and health over time. That was the only anti-perk: I was bored to death precisely because the hotel was running so well. There really weren't any challenges left. I work better when things are a mess and there are lots of challenges. I kind of thrive in chaotic situations.

At home that night I told Priscilla about the offer: "Disney has a position for me at Euro Disney in Paris. They want me to go to Orlando on Tuesday for an interview with several executives. What do you think?" You can see that I had matured in the seventeen years since I'd accepted that job in Lancaster against Priscilla's better judgment and advice . . . only to get fired ninety days later. This time around I was going to take her opinion seriously.

I expected her to say, "No! Lee, things are good here. Why take a chance? You've been with Marriott seventeen years. We have a good life."

What she said was, "Yes! Let's go."

I was shocked. "Why?" I asked her.

She said, and I will never forget her exact words, "Lee, we get to live in Paris. This is Disney, and they're going to pay you. If you don't do this, you will look back in five years and regret it!"

I said, "Okay." We literally made the decision in five minutes. The next morning, I booked the trip to Orlando. I flew down, had the round of interviews, and made the deal.

It was the first time I had ever been to the Walt Disney World Resort. Somehow, we had never taken Daniel there. We did take him to Disneyland in Anaheim when I worked in Los Angeles. He was only two at the time. Disneyland was so much fun that we would leave Daniel with a babysitter and go by ourselves. We did not tell him where we were going. I'm pleased to say he has finally forgiven us.

It's funny, looking back, how well the decision to join Disney worked out for me. A year earlier, in June 1989, Daniel called me at work in Springfield. He was on the

Disney College Program for the summer, working the front desk of Disney's Contemporary Resort. He said, "Hi, Dad. I have some bad news for you. Disney is better than Marriott!" You see, he had worked at the Copley Marriott hotel for a year during his freshman year at college.

"Why do you say that?" I asked.

He said: "Because the training is really great. It is much better than Marriott training."

That statement surprised me. I thought we at Marriott did a great job of training our associates. But now the vote was in from someone who had experienced both. The lessons here are: *You are never as good as you think you are; you can always be better; it is never too late to learn from others; and it is never too late to get better.*

I was scheduled to go to a Marriott regional management meeting with my boss and several other general managers from our region that Thursday, and here I was on Tuesday being interviewed in Orlando. That afternoon, I received a call from my secretary. She told me that the Marriott hotel in Boston, where we were supposed to have the Thursday meeting, had experienced a bad fire. The meeting was relocated to my hotel in Springfield, so I needed to get back right away to work out all the logistics with my staff.

I hopped on a plane and got back to Springfield that evening. I told my boss, Colin Nadeau, that I needed to meet with him for coffee before the meeting started on Thursday.

We met, and I resigned. I felt I needed to do it then and there because I could never get through a three-day meeting knowing I was leaving. I wanted to be the one to tell him and not have the grapevine get to him first. He had been a good leader for me, and I highly respected him.

Of course, I had second thoughts: *What have I done? Why do I keep doing these things? I don't speak French. I have never lived in Europe. Why do I keep taking these risks?* There were a million other thoughts too. I did not sleep well the next few nights as I came to grips with what Priscilla and I were about to do.

Our departure was front page news in Springfield. It was as though I was one of the first astronauts, and I was about to take the first rocket to the moon. I was not the one who attracted all the interest, though. It was Disney. If I had been leaving for another hotel company, it would have been on page 4 of the business section, not the front page. The lesson here is to never forget how powerful the Disney name is, and how respected the company is for being the best.

Priscilla was sleeping like a baby and happy as a clam after I resigned from Marriott. She had been dreaming of living in Paris for many years. I was sleeping like a baby too—I woke up every two hours and cried.

I should tell you what Priscilla said to me back in 1966, when I first met her and tried to get her to go out on a date with me. She was nineteen and working as the secretary to the director of food and beverage at the Washington Hilton hotel. I was twenty-one and a clerk in the food and beverage control office next door. She often came into my office to use our pencil sharpener, which was screwed to the metal file cabinet.

I finally asked her out. She said, "No!" She offered no alternative and no hope. She told me she had a French boyfriend, and one day she would live in France and her children would speak French and English.

I waited a few weeks and tried again: "Priscilla, what about just going for an early daylight dinner?"

She said, "No." I thought the word *daylight* would disarm her, but it didn't change her mind.

A few more months went by. Finally, I said, "Priscilla, what about just going out for a drink?"

"No."

The woman was getting on my nerves. I was not used to people saying no to me. About a year after my first try, I made another attempt. "Priscilla," I said, "what about lunch? That's all I want. No strings attached. Just lunch. After all, we work right next door to each other. What's the harm in a nice lunch?"

She said that I had a bad attitude, and she knew I wanted more than just lunch. She said the big *no* word again. I must admit I was thinking I was going to lose this one. She had never even said the word *maybe*. Later we'll discuss how "maybe" might mean "yes."

I kept asking her out, and one day she finally agreed to go to lunch . . . and that was the beginning of the end for her French boyfriend. The Frenchman already had an unfair advantage, not only because he was French but because he had a red sports car and he let Priscilla drive it. I had a red 1963 Pontiac Bonneville convertible with white leather upholstery. My mother had given it to me. It was a great car, but that little red sports car was too much competition for me. I traded in the Bonneville for a new, green two-seater Karmann Ghia (made by Volkswagen). It looked like a sports car, but it did not have the style and power of her boyfriend's car. It was all I could afford, though. I financed that car at 4 percent interest and paid $2,000 for it brand new. Inflation is real.

Twenty-four years later, in 1990, Priscilla's dream came true, but she lived in Paris for three years with me, not a French boyfriend. Today, everyone in our family but me speaks French. Daniel married a French woman, Valerie, and Priscilla's grandchildren speak French. So it all worked out just as she'd predicted back in 1966. I love this story.

Now you know why Priscilla said yes so quickly when I asked her if I should take the job with Disney. But you might be thinking to yourself, or saying to a friend or coworker, "Why did Lee tell us about his pursuit of Priscilla? What does that have to do with career development?"

Well, sometimes life lessons are also career lessons; what we learn in the course of everyday life can often be applied specifically to career development. One lesson is: If you want something, don't take no for an answer. Remember, I still had breakfast and brunch and church and many other things I could have asked Priscilla to go to with me if she had kept saying no. Patience is a virtue, for sure, and persistence is often what gets you where you want to go.

A friend of mine, Ben May, is a true salesman. He says the fun starts when the client says no. That's when the challenge begins because "No" doesn't always mean "No!" Sometimes it means "Not right now." I think far too many people give up too soon on what they want to achieve when they get a little resistance. Do not mistake an obstacle for anything other than a detour. Detours take a little longer, but you still arrive at your destination.

When I accepted the position at Disney, we put our Springfield house on the market. The housing market in New England was terrible at the time. We had hardly any prospective buyers. "It seems that we like to buy high and sell low," I lamented. There had been a bull market when we bought the house two years earlier.

I called the man who was going to replace me as general manager and told him I thought he would love my house. He and his wife looked at it and told me they thought it was too dark inside. They wanted a house with more light. It happened to be cloudy the day they visited, so I convinced the couple to come back on a bright, sunny day. They did, and we made sure to turn on every light on in the house. This time they said they liked it—but could not afford it.

I asked what they could afford. He told me. "That is exactly the price I need," I said. We lost $18,000 on that house after living in it for only two years. But my philosophy about such things is that one should cut one's losses and move on. Two years later that house was down another $20,000. As the old saying goes, "It could be worse."

Up until that time, I had not known another person who sold a house and had to bring a check to the closing—no one who will admit it, anyway. Moving often and buying houses can be a big anti-perk. If I were doing it all over today, I would rent for certain assignments.

I actually took a pay cut when I accepted the Disney job. But an adventure like that has value. Not to mention that Priscilla might have done something bad to me if I'd turned down the job over a matter of a few thousand dollars. There were also some additional perks that made up for the loss of base salary. For one thing, I was able to negotiate more stock options in lieu of a higher salary, and that turned out really well. So it was actually a fair deal because the perks and anti-perks balanced out!

Stranger in a Strange Land

I departed for the Walt Disney World Resort in Orlando for six weeks of training on July 8, 1990, after doing a thirty-day turnover with my successor in Springfield. This is way too long for a turnover, but I had such good relationships with the community and the employees that my boss asked me to stay that long. At the end of a couple of weeks, the new general manager wanted me gone, and I wanted to be gone. I acted as though I was interested in the job during those last thirty days, but it was pure performance. My heart and mind were at Disney, and I was ready to get to Paris.

I had a whirlwind training in Orlando. By the end of the six weeks, my head was spinning. I was dreaming about CRs, CTs, cannibalization, and a million other terms. I had no idea what those people at Walt Disney World were talking about. My biggest challenge was to get from one trailer to another to meet with whoever was training me. It seemed like everyone was in a trailer, which seemed quite odd to me at the time. No one can explain to you how things really work at the Walt Disney World Resort. You have to work there for a long time to figure it all out, but I can tell you this for sure: it works! Many departments were in trailers because the resort had expanded so fast that they could not build offices quickly enough.

I remember how some people presumed the strangest things. I was talking to someone one day during my training, and at the end of the session, she said, "Lee, your English is very good."

I said, "Thank you." I didn't want to say, "I certainly hope so, since I'm an American and English is the only language I speak." I think she assumed that because I was going to Euro

Disney I must be French. I found it very funny! The lesson here is to be careful about what you assume.

It rained in Orlando every afternoon that July and August, sometimes so hard that I could not believe it. I hope that rain comes back soon because every few years we end up in a drought.

Someone once said it would be great if when we were born, an instruction book came along with us that laid out exactly what was going to happen in our lives right down to the day we're going to die. I disagree. While such a system would make things much clearer, life would not be very exciting, and depending on the playbook, it could be downright discouraging. Many people achieve far more than they think they're capable of with nothing more than pure determination. Do not put limits on your dreams, and do not let anyone tell you what you can or cannot do. Write your own playbook, and fill it with high expectations for yourself.

Priscilla flew down to Orlando from Springfield for our twenty-second wedding anniversary on August 3, 1990. We celebrated at the Chefs de France restaurant at Epcot. The next week, I hired the chef of that restaurant for Euro Disney. Fourteen years later the Chefs de France restaurant added another chapter to our family history: our grandson Jullian worked there as a waiter and loved it. He was born in Paris and speaks fluent French, so he was the perfect candidate to be hired.

I really believe everyone should be a waiter or waitress at some time in their life. It's a valuable learning experience. As we've seen, I was a waiter in several places. Daniel was a waiter at Phillips Crab House in Ocean City, Maryland, and as I just mentioned, his son Jullian worked as a waiter too. Granddaughter Margot worked in food service at the Magic Kingdom, and grandson Tristan worked at the French Pavilion at Epcot. The position teaches you how to be organized, move quickly, and stay composed under pressure, and generally how to engage with all kinds of people.

I flew to Paris in early September, more or less trained in the "Disney Way." It was hard, let me tell you! My head was still spinning.

I was not totally unfamiliar with France. We had visited there often through the years with our friends Suzie and Alain Piallat, so I was not unaware of the city or the culture. Let me tell you about one of my favorite experiences. Priscilla, who speaks French, and I arrived that year on June 21, in time for an all-night music festival called Fête de Musique. It's quite a magical experience, with hundreds of musical groups performing all over France, everywhere from rooftops to sidewalks. Our friends Alain and Suzie could not join us that year, but they arranged for us to stay with Alain's father, Pascal, in his apartment in the Latin Quarter on the left bank. Pascal was a treat to stay with, and he made sure we saw the best of Paris and always had great food and wine. In fact, he bought special wine for us and would not let us drink his "ordinary wine," as he called it. He even bought a can of corn and put it in the salad one night because he'd heard that all Americans love corn. In France back then, corn was pretty much used only to feed the farm animals. Every morning, Pascal would go out and buy a baguette for lunch, and every afternoon he'd buy a fresh baguette for dinner. Food was and is a big deal in France, and Priscilla, Daniel, and I were happy to be the beneficiaries.

Pascal had attended hotel school with two other gentlemen fifty years earlier, and each of them owned a hotel in the village of Dijon in the Burgundy wine region. Of course, this is the town that made Dijon mustard famous. One morning, my family joined Pascal and some of his friends for a drive to Dijon. We had lunch at one of his old friends' hotels. We were a party of twelve. At the end of the meal they brought out a cheese trolley with at least forty different cheeses on it. This was another world from my childhood in Oklahoma, where the range of cheeses was Velveeta, Swiss, Cheddar, and American. Brie did not get to Oklahoma until long after I was gone, and even then Americans would heat it up in the oven and have it as an hors d'oeuvre.

It was a spectacular lunch in a beautiful hotel restaurant in a quaint village—memorable, to say the least. Priscilla was in heaven, as she adores all cheeses. After lunch, we drove out into the Burgundy wine country and stopped at a couple of vineyards, where the entire French contingent had a lot of conversation with the local owners. But after a couple of stops, we still had not been offered any wine to taste. I wasn't sure what was going on because I didn't understand a word of French. At one stop, one of the ladies in the wine cellar spoke

English, so I asked her what the best recent vintages of wine were in Burgundy. She told me that the 1976 and 1978 were superb, the best in several years. That small bit of information would save my life, or at least my self-respect, within the hour, proving once again the value of asking questions.

We went to the next vineyard, as they were one after another for kilometer after kilometer. The vineyards are narrow and run up the sloping hills. It is an absolutely beautiful site. When we arrived at the next vineyard and got out of our cars, we were greeted by a tanned, handsome Frenchman. It took three to four minutes for all of the greetings and kissing to take place. If you're a regular friend, you get kissed once on each cheek, and you have to kiss everyone else on both cheeks as well . . . and if you are a really special friend, the kisses move to three for each person. I think there is a category for four kisses, but I never learned what it was. I like this tradition, and we have adopted it in our family since we can now claim French relatives.

The first thing our host did was to ask Daniel what he would like to drink. He said a Coke, of course. They did not have Coke, so they served him a Pepsi, of all things. He was happy. When you're twelve you don't need much to make you happy. He had already survived a French lunch earlier in the day. He was not offered a children's menu and, therefore, got no macaroni and cheese, or hot dogs, or chicken fingers. This was before McDonald's arrived in France. Today, most kids in France want to go to McDonald's just as they do here in the United States.

We all proceeded into a small wine cellar with gravel on the floor and a few very large wooden barrels of wine stacked around the room. The cellar was dark, lighted only by a single light bulb hanging from the ceiling. Everyone was talking and having a grand time. The owner let each of us try a sip of the wine that was fermenting in the large wooden casks to see how it was progressing. Suddenly there was a roar of laughter from the French group. They had been talking together and, of course, I had no clue what they were talking about. I learned in a minute that they had told the owner that I was an American hotelman and a food and beverage expert.

He said something to the group in French, and they all stared at me with semiserious smiles on their faces. I said to our friend Pascal, "What did he say?"

He told me that our host had said, "So let's see how much the American hotelman knows about wine." I was at that moment wishing I had some cyanide pills to crush between my teeth, but I did not, so I smiled and acted as if it were no big deal.

Our host went into the back and brought out the largest Burgundy wine glasses I had ever seen. They each looked like they would hold a full bottle or two of wine. He then returned to the back and brought out a dusty bottle of red Burgundy wine. (There are white Burgundies too, by the way.) He handled the bottle in a very gentle and careful way, like a father with a newborn baby. He wiped it and cleaned it up before taking his corkscrew and opening it. He then looked at me with what I perceived as a wicked smile, but I could have been wrong since I was in the middle of a nervous breakdown. I could hear my heart beating and was glad that they couldn't hear it.

You see, my wife and son were watching, and I was thinking I was about to be humiliated in front of nine Frenchmen who knew more about wine when they were in the first grade than I did after all my years in the industry. The thought of being embarrassed in front of Priscilla did not bother me all that much. She's always known that I don't know everything. But my son *did* think I knew everything, and he was about to see me humiliated in front of all those people.

Our host gently poured about two ounces of wine into one of the gigantic glasses and handed it to me. I held it up to the light and swirled it around for about fifteen seconds. I acted as if I were studying it carefully for the heaviness of the wine as it slipped down the glass in a wavelike motion. This is called "ropes." I had learned about it back in my wine class at the Waldorf Astoria ten years earlier. The slower the wine drifts down the glass, the more body it has. I said, "Good ropes."

Our French friend translated, and there was a glimmer of respect from the faces of the onlookers. It was very quiet as I brought the glass to my nose while continuing to swirl it around to check the aroma. It smelled quite good. I said, "Good nose."

I took what seemed like a long time before I looked at the wine again. Then I put a small amount in my mouth and sucked it over my tongue just as we had learned to do in class. I swirled it in my mouth while looking up, as if I were contemplating what vintage the wine was. Of course, I had no idea, but I did know it was a very good wine. I had learned to tell the difference between great wines and mediocre wines, and I was sure from the way our host handled the bottle that he was serving me something special.

I waited a few more seconds before taking one more taste. "This is a seventy-eight Burgundy," I said. "No, wait, It's a seventy-six Burgundy."

Our host immediately said, in an excited voice, "Voilà!" which kind of means "You got it." In a flash, everyone in the room was congratulating me with handshakes and kisses. I saw the look of pride on Daniel's face and the look of disbelief on Priscilla's. I had done it. It was a great guess! I did not tell Priscilla and Daniel the truth until we got home three weeks later, as I wanted to savor my new fame. I told them I had used the information the lady at one of the vineyards had given me about the recent great vintages. It was a calculated guess, I suppose you could say.

That left a lasting impression on my son. When he was in the twelfth grade, he wrote an essay on how his dad had saved the pride of America in France. He started the essay with the notion that most French people think Americans only know about McDonald's and Coca-Cola, and his dad had proved them wrong on that bright, sunny day in Burgundy. In his essay, I was an American hero.

I learned that if you keep calm and cool and think clearly, you can guess the truth—or get really close to it just by taking your time and asking questions along the way. They would have been impressed if I had stuck with my first guess of 1978. For all I knew, it was an 1878 or a 1962 wine, but the lady in the wine cellar had told me about the best vintages. The real lesson here is that when you ask questions and take the time to listen to people, and you respect their thoughts and perspectives, what you learn can be a springboard to success.

All the experiences I'd had in my previous trips to France over the years, like that day of wine tasting, made a big difference in my comfort level when I arrived in Paris to begin my new job. It was a Sunday morning, and I was supposed to be picked up at Charles de Gaulle Airport by the vice president of Euro Disney. The HR department in Orlando had faxed my flight number and my picture to him.

Do you know what faxed photos looked like back then? They looked like gray, black, and white blobs. The picture of me could have been a picture of anything you can imagine. As a result, the person picking me up could not spot me. I waited for him for about an hour. When we finally got together, he dropped me at my temporary apartment and handed me the keys to my company car and a map to the office for the next morning. Then he left. I was exhausted, not only from the flight but from the stress of thinking about what I was about to get into. *I now live in France!* That was a sudden and scary thought. *I'm alone, and I don't speak French.* Priscilla could speak French but wasn't coming for two more weeks.

I took a nap. Sleep and hot water are two great healers, in my opinion, for both physical and mental pain. When I woke up at about 4:00 p.m., I was hungry, so I walked down to the Avenue de Vincennes, which is a large boulevard with cafes and stores everywhere. You can't imagine how intimidated I was by the French. I could hardly even say "Bonjour!" Actually, I could say it, but I was afraid that if I did people might think I spoke French, and then what would I do when they threw a bunch of other French words back to me? Better to just keep quiet, I decided.

I went into a shop that had a sandwich case. I spotted a ham-and-cheese sandwich. I actually did know the word for ham, *jambon*, and cheese, *fromage*. I ran those two words through my mind a couple of times and finally said, "Madame, jambon et fromage, s'il vous plaît." I was happy when she smiled and gave me that sandwich. I said, "Merçi." It was nice to realize that I knew at least nine French words. That was a big deal. I had done it. I was not going to starve before Priscilla arrived.

I gave the store clerk twenty francs and hoped that what she gave me in return was the correct change. I wondered, *What are all these coins worth?* This was long before the euro became the standard European currency.

Before long I was able to order a beer, a wine, a coffee, and so on. I discovered that I actually knew more French words than I thought I did, so the variety of my diet expanded after about two weeks of jambon et fromage sandwiches. Remember *croissant*—this is a very good word for breakfast. By the time I left France, I still could not speak French, but I knew a lot of French words and I was able to get by because I was no longer intimidated.

It's amazing how you can be afraid of something and then, before long, be totally comfortable with it. The lesson here is: *Never underestimate what you can do if you put your mind to it, even if you're thrown into a difficult situation you hadn't counted on.* Everything is hard before it's easy, but when you do the hard things, life gets easier and more exciting.

Within a couple of weeks, I was driving like a Frenchman and could find my way into and out of Paris without any problem at all. That's one thing I love about the cities I've lived in: I know my way around them now. I feel at home in all of them, even today.

One of the nice things about France is that the French people do not carry on small talk with you in stores and cafes the way Americans do. You order your coffee; they give you your coffee. You ask for the check; they give you the check. They don't ask where you're from, or tell you a joke, or anything else, and that was just fine with me. I did not want to talk with them, because I couldn't! I feel sorry for someone who comes to the United States not speaking

English. It must be a nightmare because here, anybody and everybody tries to talk to you about this or that.

I left for work early on my first Monday morning, to give myself time in case I got lost. The office was supposedly only fifteen minutes away, but it was France, and my first day on the job, so I was not taking any chances. But the map I was given worked just fine, and I arrived at work an hour early. No one else was there. I quickly learned that if you wanted coffee, you needed a two-franc coin to get it out of a machine. In France, nothing at work is free, and the coffee was not your ordinary Maxwell House. We're talking high-test stuff here.

The days were very stressful in the beginning. Everything was different. Even making a phone call seemed hard. I would call someplace, and the person who answered did not speak English. Since I didn't speak French, I would think, *What do I do now*? What I promptly did was get a secretary who spoke both French and English. Her name was Susan Defosse. She was from the United Kingdom, and she was great. She had the same kind of sarcastic sense of humor I had, so we got along "jolly well."

Priscilla arrived and found us an apartment on the east side of Paris, twenty-five minutes from work. It was a small thousand-square-foot place with no closets in the bedrooms, so we converted one of the bedrooms into a closet. The location was great, right next to a beautiful park and the Château de Vincennes, which took up two square blocks and had a huge moat around it. It took two centuries to complete its construction—and you thought that some of your projects took a long time to complete! It was quite neat living next to this beautiful château. If you're ever in Paris, it is well worth taking the time to go see it. Just take the M1 Metro east to the end of the line, get off, and there it is.

On one of my days off, I was sitting on a bench near the park, reading. A car stopped, and one of the occupants asked me in French for directions to the zoo. I was shocked that I understood what she said, and even more shocked that I was able to give her directions in French. That was a big deal to me. It did not happen often, so I was pretty excited. Isn't it funny what can make you happy in life?

Over the next three years, we had a lot of visits from friends and family, just as we do now in Orlando. When we lived in Springfield, we had few visitors. Was it Paris or us that they wanted to see? I always wondered!

We had house rules for visitors:

- *Do not complain about your feet; we will be doing a lot of walking.*

- *We will exchange your money for you once; after that, you have to do it yourself.*

- *We will show you how to use the Metro once, and then you are on your own.*

- *Do not take long showers because we do not have much hot water.*

- *Eat what is on your plate when we go to a restaurant, and do not make an ugly face when you learn what the stuff on your plate is.*

- *Be polite and say "bonjour" to our neighbors, because we have to live here after you are gone.*

Life was really good for the next two years before Euro Disney opened. The park had no guests to worry about yet, and no cast members either. Last but not least, we didn't have to worry about making a profit yet. Preopening is a sweet time.

For the first nine months, I recruited management, traveling all over the world interviewing candidates. That was one of great perks, as I got to see all kinds of places I'd never been to before. I eventually hired 225 managers for food and beverage operations. A lot of them were Europeans who were living in the United States but wanted to return to Europe, especially if they could work for Disney. Many of the people I hired are still at the Walt Disney World Resort today, doing outstanding jobs in various leadership roles. They are some of Disney's best people. Others are spread around the world doing great work for other organizations.

Dieter Hannig was Euro Disney's head of concept development for food and beverage operations when I arrived in Paris. That was the first time I met him. Little did we know that we would work together for a long time at Euro Disney, and then for many years at Walt Disney World in Orlando. Dieter is by far one of the best food and beverage professionals in the world; he's the single reason the food at Disney World rose from good to great. Lesson: *Hiring the best always pays off.*

I learned many lessons from the leaders I hired. One lesson on persistence came from a woman named Nora Carey. She was an American who had been living in London and wanted to work for Disney in Paris. She had lots of skills in menu planning, menu design, cooking, teaching, and many other areas, but unfortunately I had no position for her on my staff, so I had to tell her no. She kept trying, and I kept saying no.

One day, I received in the mail an invitation to a reception at the Ritz Hotel in Paris in honor of Julia Child, the famous American food connoisseur, author, and host of a popular TV cooking show. I RSVP'd that Priscilla and I would attend.

Side note for those who sometimes don't respond when an invitation says RSVP: it stands for the French *Répondez s'il vous plaît*. It literally means "Respond if it pleases you." But the "if it pleases you" part is not meant literally. Many people think it means you should respond only if you are going to attend, while others think it means respond if you're *not*. In fact, the customary meaning is please respond whether you are coming or not. Sometimes we get a call from someone saying, "We are RSVP-ing to your party." We then say, "Are you coming, or are you not coming?"

It's quite unprofessional and shows a lack of manners not to respond properly to an invitation that says RSVP. This is important; you don't want to get an invitation from your boss and handle it improperly. It's kind of like drinking from the finger bowl, or using the wrong utensil, or not putting your napkin in your lap. If you are unsure, watch the other diners, and go last.

Back to the story at the Ritz. As we were going through the receiving line, we came to Julia Child, and who should be standing next to her doing the introductions? Nora Carey! Nora said, "Julia, I would like you to meet the director of food and beverage for Euro Disney, Lee Cockerell."

Julia looked down at me, because she was quite tall, "Mr. Cockerell," she said, "I hope the food is going to be better here than it is in Orlando."

I can't remember what I said. I think I grunted something like "Me too." Her point was that food is a much more serious thing in France than it is in America.

The story has a happy ending. Years later, Julia came to Walt Disney World to attend the food-and-wine festival. By then, Dieter Hannig had been in charge of our food and beverage business for some time. I'm pleased to report that Julia told me, "Mr. Cockerell, the food is really good here now. I take back what I said to you back in Paris a few years ago."

The real point of this story is that Nora Carey found another way to get to me. We ended up hiring her to manage all of our graphic work for the resorts, including the menus and a million other things. Thank goodness we did because Nora was excellent. We created a job for her, and it turned out to be one we really needed, only we didn't realize it until she convinced us! That is one story about the value of persistence; another one is in the paragraphs below.

After the managers were all hired and on their way to Paris, Priscilla and I had time to take some nice vacations in Europe and other locations. In 1991, we went to India and Nepal with my boss, Sanjay Varma, and his wife, Hanny. Sanjay is Indian, which made the trip even better. There were only about ten people on the flight to India because the Gulf War had started only three days earlier and we had to fly around Iraq. The trip was a big perk. India is a fascinating place and quite exotic.

I experienced another great example of persistence in India and also learned the true meaning of the word "maybe." We were in the ancient city of Benares (now Varanasi), walking along the Ganges River at six o'clock one morning, about to take a boat ride. By that time, we were numb from all the beggars who came up to us. The poverty is really hard to imagine. It was common to see people living on the sidewalks. A young man approached Priscilla and tried to sell her some handmade trinkets. She tried to put him off, but he was quite insistent. She finally said just two words to him: "Maybe later."

We boarded the boat and floated out on the Ganges River, which is very holy in the Hindu religion. For centuries, people have come to Benares to die and be cremated on the banks of the river. Cremations go on all day long. We had a great boat trip for a few miles. It was quite something to watch the city awaken, with people doing laundry in the river or selling their goods, with cremations in progress, cows wandering the streets, and beggars everywhere. In India, you can buy beggar coins. For a dollar you get a handful of coins that may be worth 2 cents each. It's a necessary system; without it you would be broke in a few minutes with so many people begging. I never once felt unsafe, though. Their religion helps them cope with the poverty they find themselves in. They are a wonderful people.

We got off that boat several miles down the river, and what did we see? The young man who had approached Priscilla an hour before to sell his goods. He had walked along the bank, following our boat all the way. Once again he approached Priscilla and asked her to buy some of his things. She said, "No. I am not interested."

He said, "But, madam, you said maybe later." His persistence paid off. She made a purchase! Great lesson here! "Maybe later" to him meant "Yes." When you are in business or personal negotiations, listen carefully to every word. Also ask yourself if you're persistent enough when you want something and meet resistance.

Preopening Pressure

Our life was really great in 1990, and it continued that way through September 1991. The real work began in October. That's when the pace picked up; we were only seven months away from opening and we had one deadline after another to meet. Adding to the pressure were these factors:

- *We had to do everything in five languages: English, French, German, Italian, and Spanish.*

- *There was no "Disney Culture" yet in France. We were responsible for putting in place that famous culture of excellence, courtesy, friendliness, and attention to detail.*

- *We were having meeting after meeting from six in the morning until evening, and sometimes past midnight.*

On an average day, during those last seven months before opening, I would get up at four in the morning and get to work by 4:45. There is zero traffic at that time. Then I would usually work until around 10:00 p.m. That is, on average, a seventeen-hour day. I would get home at 10:30 p.m., fall into bed, and get up again at 4:00 a.m. That went on for seven months, six or seven days a week. When people tell you they work eighteen hours a day, be skeptical. I surprised myself. I did not know I had that kind of stamina!

I had quit drinking alcohol a year before opening. It was tough since I love wine and was living in France where some of the best wines in the world are produced. But I needed every single ounce of energy. I did nothing but sleep and work for seven months.

Well, I also ate, but not much. I packed one or two peanut butter and jelly sandwiches every day because I was starving by 9:00 or 10:00 a.m. I would have one sandwich then and another for my second lunch. I guarantee you that if you make a peanut butter and jelly sandwich, wrap it in foil, and forget about it, it will still be fine a week later. They really stay moist. I would often find in my briefcase an old sandwich I'd forgotten about, and I'd eat it days after it was made. That high-energy, tasty, healthy sandwich also saves a lot of time. It was so important to me that we had friends bring or mail peanut butter to us because they did not sell it in France. Later, when I started working at Disney World in Orlando, I again brought those sandwiches with me. I had forgotten how good they were and how much time I saved by having them with me.

I kidded Priscilla when I got home one night. I said, "Did you get up today?"

"What do you mean?" she asked.

"Well, you were in bed when I left this morning, and you're in bed now." This was somewhat amusing to her, but I could do it only once.

Priscilla was a trouper. She did her thing in Paris and never said a word about all the hours I was working. She had been through openings with me before and knew how they worked. And she loved Paris. I think she went to a different part of the city every day for three years. Shopping for ordinary household goods took up a big part of her day, and she did not have a car. Little things like getting your dry cleaning done were different there. When you pick up a suit from the cleaners, they don't give you the hanger. They take it off the hanger and fold it up—cost savings in action. You also bag your own groceries, so you usually bring your own bag with you. This is forced waste reduction and labor-cost reduction in action.

One custom we never really got used to in France was restaurants opening for dinner at 8:00 p.m. We often arrived exactly at that hour, and the servers and cooks would still be sitting in the dining room having their own dinner. Most guests did not arrive until 9:00 or 10:00 p.m. Also, we had to learn to trick the servers because they would not serve us coffee until we had eaten our dessert, as is the custom in France. We would tell the waiter we did not want dessert, and we would order coffee, and then as soon as the coffee arrived, we would say we'd changed our mind and would like a dessert after all. That way we could have our coffee and dessert together.

Another thing we had to learn was that servers do not come over to take an order until the patrons have closed their menus. This is the signal that one is ready to order. We also learned that wine is served only with food. One does not order a glass of wine as a cocktail or drink it before dinner. On the other hand, champagne is okay at any time and for any reason. That's just the way it is, whether you like it or not.

Priscilla walked me around our neighborhood in Vincennes and introduced me to all the shopkeepers where she shopped and told them I did not speak French. She would send me to the store to get things with a note for me to hand the shopkeeper, just as a little kid would do. That was weird until I got used to it. At least with that system, I would bring home the right cheese.

La Grande Ouverture

We were finally ready for the grand opening. The Euro Disney Resort officially opened at 9:00 a.m. on April 12, 1992.

Well, you're never as ready as you wish you were, so there were lots of problems to solve immediately. It felt like the building of the pyramids in Egypt. There were thousands of cast members doing everything you could imagine. I had never seen anything like it. It was of mammoth proportions.

We had an opening-night party for ten thousand people. It was a sight to behold. We bought virtually every shrimp in Europe, and every strawberry too. We poured more champagne than I have ever seen in one place. The cost of food for the party exceeded $1 million. We could not have pulled it off without the help of a great task force from the Walt Disney World Resort. There were hundreds of them. It was like the Allied landing at Normandy in World War II. Among the group were Meg Crofton and Don Robinson and many other people I would later work with in Orlando. Craig Hodges and Djuan Rivers ran the bell station, which was a tent where they checked in and out ten thousand pieces of guest luggage without losing a single piece.

The grand opening went perfectly, and as the night ended we were all thrilled with the great work we had done. We finally went to bed around 4:00 a.m. We were all geared up and staffed up to take on the huge crowds that were forecast for the summer. We were ready. We had thought of everything. It was sure to be one of the greatest experiences of my life.

But a funny thing happened: no one came.

A combination of two factors was responsible for keeping people away: there was a serious recession in Europe, and there had been too much negative press about how busy it would be. As a result, we were overstaffed by about two thousand cast members. They were all on contracts that would take at least ninety days to break, and it would be costly to break them.

I called it "the summer from Hades." I do not know what heaven is like; but after that summer, I knew what the alternative was like . . . and I never wanted to go there again. Between the park and the resorts, we were losing $1 million a day, each and every day. You can't imagine what the pressure is like when you're losing a million every twenty-four hours. We had many visits from Michael Eisner, the CEO of The Walt Disney Company, and Frank Wells, the president. These were not pleasant visits, to say the least.

It was like being on the *Titanic*, except instead of water rushing in, French francs were rushing out. We knew that not everyone was going to get out alive (professionally speaking).

What we would go through after 9/11 at Disney World was, from a business perspective, like child's play compared to what we had to deal with in France. We had a wonderful product with great hotels, a great park, great food, and great cast members. The only thing missing was guests, and of course the one really important thing: revenue! It was the most difficult job I've ever had, including the one many years earlier that ended with me getting fired.

A lot of managers and executives were biting the dust, or maybe I should say jumping overboard. The pressure was overwhelming. People were quitting, resigning, getting fired, and everything else you could think of. Divorces were happening left and right. Wives were moving back to wherever they came from; the kids were crying. It was not fun. Does this paint a good picture for you of how bad things can be? Missing a merit increase or having your hours reduced would have been like a promotion compared to what we were dealing with. We sometimes reorganized twice a week. All of our preparation was of little use, as we had to immediately change many of our concepts, processes, and procedures when the few guests who did show up taught us what they wanted.

I had been through difficult experiences many times in my career, so I was able to stay cool, calm, and collected. I focused on doing the best I could with what I had to work with. Barry Jacobson, Mark Mrozinski, Carolyn Argo, Rick Allen, Val Bunting, Dave Vermeulen, Mark Mannella, Greg Wann, Barbara Higgins, Kim Marinaccio, and others who were on the task force could also tell you how tough things can really be. They were on the same roller coaster I was on. Even Pam Landwirth, the current president of Give Kids the World, was there with us working day and night. I think we had ninety thousand test-meal coupons to give out so we could practice in the restaurants before opening to the public.

Thankfully, I did not get fired. In fact, three months after the opening I was promoted to vice president of Euro Disney Resorts. I replaced the previous vice president, who had left on the last lifeboat. I was responsible for the operations of the six-thousand-room resorts. I don't think I would have been able to get that promotion if I had not had the experience of being a general manager of a hotel before, at Marriott. That little move to Springfield a few years earlier had paid off. *Experience eventually starts to pay you back in real money.*

We continued on and did the best we could. The problems never went away, and didn't really get much smaller, but you can get used to any circumstances. So, after a while, we had days off and went on vacations just like normal people.

Today we would say we adjusted to "the new normal." But there's actually no such thing as "new normal" as far as I'm concerned. All there is is what is—and leaders need to learn how to adjust to current circumstances instead of standing around wishing, hoping, whining, and praying that things will get back to how they used to be, or how they would like them to be. The key is to put your head down and start the painful work of getting things to be what you want them to be instead of how they are at the moment, and this can take time.

We were in a tough set of circumstances, and I just did the best I could because that was all I could do. I learned more about myself during that opening than I ever had before or since. After opening Euro Disney, I knew I could hold up under any pressure that came my way, and when I moved to Orlando to work at the Walt Disney World Resort, it seemed like heaven.

To make matters worse, my father-in-law, Admiral Charles Payne, died in February 1993. In his desk was a note card with these words: "Do your best, and then forgive yourself." That's really all any of us can do. If you're doing your best, you have nothing to be ashamed of. And it's important to remember that what really matters is not so much what happens to us but how we react to what happens to us. Leaders have to stay cool, calm, and collected no matter what. Everyone is watching.

We flew home from France to attend my father-in-law's memorial service, which was held at the United States Naval Academy in Annapolis, Maryland. Everyone said wonderful things about him. One thing that was said would affect our lives back in Paris a couple of weeks later. More on that in a minute.

The minister was talking about Charlie Payne's successes in his life, from growing up poor in Arkansas, to fighting in World War II, to graduating from the Massachusetts Institute of Technology and the Naval Academy, to becoming an admiral in the United States Navy. The minister was talking about his drive and determination to go after and achieve what he wanted. The minister went on to say that Charlie had told Sunshine, his wife, on their first date when they were sixteen, that he was going to marry her. Sunshine said she thought he was a nut, but seven years later they were married. The message the minister left us with was that Charlie Payne did not wait to take the safe or cautious route to anything. He took immediate action!

Back in the 1960s, a navy officer by the name of Lloyd Bucher let the North Koreans board his vessel, the *Pueblo*, off the coast of North Korea. The North Koreans had alleged that the ship was inside the twelve-mile limit. I remember Charlie telling me that Bucher should never have let the North Koreans board that ship.

"What should he have done?" I asked.

He replied: "They should have fought to the death."

I remember asking him when he first knew that he was willing to die for his country. He said it was the day he became a naval officer and swore to the Constitution of the United States of America to defend the freedom of America. He said, "Lee, you have to decide what you stand for long before an incident happens so you will be ready to react quickly and appropriately."

This is true for all kinds of ethical issues that leaders are faced with every day, and this is what I learned—be ready to do the right thing! Remember, the newspaper is full of stories every day that showcase examples of leaders who made the wrong choices. By the way, the *Pueblo* is the only captured US naval vessel in the history of the United States that is still held by a foreign power. It is currently a tourist attraction in North Korea.

After the memorial service, Daniel and I flew back to Paris on his birthday, which we celebrated in flight, while Priscilla stayed behind to help her mother, Sunshine, get things squared away. It was a long, overnight flight, and I thought a lot about how fragile and unpredictable life is.

Daniel and I went back to work at Disneyland Paris. One night about a week later, I was the executive on duty for the resort. The executive on duty held that responsibility for one week, staying in one of the hotels so he or she would be available for any emergencies twenty-four hours a day.

I got a call about 8:00 p.m. from Daniel. He was in the lobby of the hotel and wanted to see me. I said, "Sure. Come on up." That was not normal behavior for him, so I was a little concerned about what he was coming to tell me.

When he walked in the door, I was not sure what was going to happen, but I could already feel that whatever it was, it was a big one. I knew that because of the determined look on his face, which I have since seen many times over the years. I knew he was not there to ask for my advice or my permission for anything, and I knew he was not there to borrow money.

This is what I referred to when I described the minister saying that Charlie Payne, Daniel's grandfather, always acted on his feelings and had a lot of drive and determination, and it was going to affect our lives in a couple of weeks. Daniel had huge love and respect for his grandfather, and he had heard what that minister said. It had affected him.

"Hi, what's up?" I said.

He replied, "Valerie and I are getting married." He had learned from Priscilla to get to the point and use few words.

Yep, it was a big one! I was thrilled. We had known Valerie for some time, and we thought she was terrific. "Congratulations, that is wonderful," I said. "So where is Valerie?"

He said, "She's in the lobby."

"Well, go get her so we can call your mother and Sunshine to tell them the good news."

Priscilla had predicted back in 1991 that we would have a French daughter-in-law when Daniel moved to France after college. I asked her why she predicted that. Her answer was: "Lee, you fall in love where you live, and your son is twenty-two and living in Paris."

It was 2:00 p.m. in the United States, so I promptly picked up the phone and called Priscilla to tell her that her son was getting married. She said, "I knew he was. I could feel it during my dad's memorial service."

I thought, *How do women do that*? I had not picked up any vibes at all, and back in 1991 I had never thought that Daniel would marry a French woman. *How do women do that*? I want to learn this.

Priscilla has told me a couple of times that my awareness of what is going on around me is low. I think she may be on to something. I joke with her from time to time by telling her it's not my fault. We men are just a billion or so years behind women, and one day we will catch up. Evolution has been a little slower for us, I tell her, and it's not our fault! I don't think I've convinced her.

Once again you may be asking yourself, "Why is Lee telling us all of this? What does this have to do with career development?" I'll tell you later how it all comes together nicely and makes perfect sense under the heading "career magic." You will see how life puts you through experiences and situations that don't make sense at the time, but how, in the end, things can turn out perfectly. It's how the game ends that's important, not whether you're behind during the game.

We are now up to March 1993 in my story. I had been working for twenty-eight years. Priscilla and I had moved ten times since we were married twenty-four years prior. I was in my twenty-first job and about to become a father-in-law. I considered the position of father-in-law a significant promotion in my life, right after husband and father.

I estimate that the previous three years contributed at least $3 million to my experience account; all together I had accumulated $10 million in experience. And now another unexpected great ride was about to happen on the Big Career Roller Coaster. I'll tell you about that next.

Insights

Take the risk.

Boredom and regret are deadly.

The most important decision you make is the life partner you choose.

To get what you want, be persistent.

The power of exposure to other cultures is huge.

Hire the best talent.

Buckle down and get the job done . . . you can rest later.

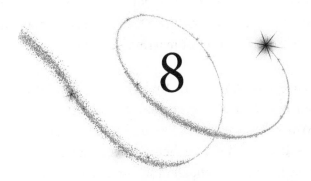

The Magical Disney World Years: 1993–2006

When we went to France in 1990, I expected to be there at least five years. By March 1993, when Daniel told me he and Valerie were getting married, we had been there only three. I had not been fired, even though the company was losing a great deal of money, so I figured I was safe, at least for a while. Actually, I never even thought about losing my job. I'm not sure why it didn't cross my mind, but it never did, even though it probably should have. But by that time, I was a business-war veteran! I would have won the Purple Heart if one was awarded in business, as I had been wounded many times in my career and survived. Some of my wounds were physical, but most were mental.

The wedding date for Valerie and Daniel was set for April 24, 1993. In France, when someone gets married, they have the ceremony in the town hall of the village they live in, and the mayor officiates. Daniel and Valerie were going to get married in Tigeaux, the small village they lived in at the time, a short distance from Euro Disney. He is probably the only American who ever got married in that village.

Valerie's father, Victor, told Daniel that the first American he'd ever met gave him a chocolate bar at the end of World War II, and the second one he met was now taking his daughter away. In fact, he loves Daniel, the father of his three grandchildren, all of whom live in America. He is luckier than I am in that he also has three grandchildren in France. I thought Victor's comment was pretty neat for someone to be able to say. I remember seeing movies of American soldiers giving out chocolate bars to the kids when they were liberating France.

With the wedding only a few weeks away, arrangements were made for all of us to get together so the two families could meet. Valerie's parents drove up to Paris from their home in a small village near Lyon. We all gathered one Wednesday night and had a wonderful evening together. One thing I love about France is that they open a bottle of champagne for every celebration, no matter how big or small.

Priscilla translated for four hours. Victor and I just drank our champagne and smiled since he did not speak English and I did not speak French. Priscilla and Valerie's mother, Anna, kept up the conversation all evening as Victor and I just nodded from time to time and enjoyed our champagne. After that evening together, and then the marriage, we had some new traditions in our family. When any of us went to

France, I would send a bottle of California wine along for Victor, and he would send me back a bottle of French wine.

At Thanksgiving, we added a cheese course to the menu in honor of our French daughter-in-law, Valerie. If you've ever wondered why some dishes served at your home on holidays are unique to your family, look back to see who married whom and where they were from. Ask your grandparents; they probably know the history of that dish. Grandparents are wise and know everything.

As you probably know, the French make lots of jokes about Americans, and in return Americans make lots of jokes about the French. It's funny how, when you have a French daughter-in-law and three perfect, adorable, half-French grandchildren, you don't find those jokes amusing in the least. The lesson is we should not joke about other people. There are many reasons for that, and a big one is that one of them might become part of your family. This is your diversity lesson for the day, and one I have learned well.

Speaking about tradition, I thought I would never have to pay for a wedding because I had a son and not a daughter. Well, I quickly learned that in France, the custom is for the two families to share the cost of the wedding. It was a tiny anti-perk, but well worth it.

Daniel and Valerie had what I think was the perfect wedding. It was a Saturday afternoon, and they were married by the assistant mayor of Tigeaux in the village's town hall. The mayor was supposed to marry them, but his wife died the day before the wedding and the assistant mayor had to step in. They were not married in a church because Daniel was not Catholic. If he had been, they would have had two ceremonies: one religious and one legal.

After the ceremony, we went to the couple's home and had cake and, of course, champagne! That evening, the wedding party, which was made up of twenty family members and friends, went to the Jules Verne restaurant in the Eiffel Tower for a wonderful dinner. Then, on Sunday, there was a big reception for friends, family, and coworkers. The reason I say it was perfect is that we were able to spend an evening with just the bride and groom, their families, and their closest friends, which is not possible when you have one of those huge receptions right after the ceremony, where the parents barely get to see their sons or daughters. Remember the movie *The Father of the Bride*?

Meanwhile, a couple of weeks after Daniel and Valerie announced their upcoming marriage, I got a call from my boss, Sanjay, telling me that Al Weiss wanted to talk with me about a job in Orlando at Walt Disney World. I asked when the job would be available. Sure enough, it was available right away. I made sure everyone understood that I could not start any new job until after my son's wedding on April 24.

But I did fly to Orlando to interview with Al Weiss, the new executive vice president of Walt Disney World Resorts. I didn't make it to Orlando the day I was supposed to arrive because we couldn't land in Atlanta to change planes, thanks to the biggest snowstorm ever to hit the East Coast. Our flight was diverted to Dallas, where I spent two days in a dumpy motel before I could get a flight to Orlando.

Al and I had our interview, and he offered me the job. I headed back to Paris for the wedding and to tie up loose ends and prepare to move. It was agreed that I would start in May, after the wedding. I liked Al right away because when I told him I like to work out around 5:30 p.m. every day and I didn't want him to see I wasn't in my office at that time and think I wasn't committed to my job, he said he really believes in balance and that he too was often away, coaching his daughter's baseball team or his son's basketball team. He said he would never miss any of their school events or games. The more he talked, the more I loved the man. Where had he been all my life? One lesson here is: *Make sure you do everything possible to ensure that those around you are able to attend those special family events.*

Back in Paris, they had already held the management going-away party for me, but they planned another one—a Saturday afternoon event in early May at my boss's house. A large group was invited, including the husbands, wives, and kids of my coworkers. All events, in my opinion, are more fun when children are present. Unfortunately, I ended up missing both parties.

Al Weiss called and told me to fly back to Orlando for a meeting, where it would be announced that I would be the new senior vice president for Walt Disney World Resorts operations. He wanted me to be there when the announcement was made so I could immediately meet with the team and they would know who I was. My intention was to fly over, attend the announcement meeting, and get right back to Paris for the Saturday afternoon going-away party.

I flew over with no problems. We made the announcement. I was all ready to fly back to Paris for the party and to start getting ready to move a couple of weeks later. Well, that was a good plan, but my flight had equipment problems and I spent the next day and night in Raleigh, North Carolina. The party in Paris went on without me, the guest of honor, in attendance. I managed to attend for ten minutes by telephone. Just another normal day on the Big Career/Life Roller Coaster.

In The Magic Kingdom

I started at the Walt Disney World Resort on May 23, 1993, as senior vice president of operations for the hotels. Priscilla stayed behind in Paris and joined me in Orlando in June. Daniel stayed in France with his new wife, of course. I was now forty-eight years old, and I'd been working for twenty-eight years. It was our eleventh move in twenty-five years of marriage. We never thought we would live in Orlando, and we're still there. You just never know where that Big Career/Life Roller Coaster is going to take you.

Meg Crofton, who until 2015 was president of Disney Parks and Resorts for the US and France, and Dale Stafford, who recently retired from Disney after many, many years, were going to be vice presidents of resort operations, reporting to me. As soon as I met them, we started putting together a new organizational structure. In those days, the resorts, parks, and all support operations were run separately, each with its own executive team. That was far different than it is today. Now, Disney World's organizational structure enables all areas to work together in order to move more quickly and run the Walt Disney World Resort as one place with one team!

The very first thing we had to deal with was a business downturn. We were in a lot of meetings thinking about numerous ways to save money. We came up with lots of good ideas that are still in place today. For example, we decided not to change the sheets every day since the guests could not have cared less and it also helped with environmental issues; we used much less water and ran a lot fewer chemicals down the drain. We also eliminated many layers of management, such as resident managers, executive chefs, and food and beverage managers in the resorts. Disney World can thank me for putting in an email system in 1993, shortly after I got there. The Walt Disney World Resort did not have email at the time, even though we had it in France. Come to think of it, some people might thank me and others curse me; once you get used to having email it's hard to get along without it.

I started teaching time management right away as a forum for people to get to know me. I scheduled several evening meetings for two hundred to three hundred managers so they could see my face and hear my philosophy. I had them fax in questions they wanted me to answer because that email system was not in place yet. They sent me lots of tough questions, and I answered every one of them. I wanted to get all the rumors and guessing out of the way.

I guess it was the forerunner of what Disney now calls the New Leader Transition sessions, which all leaders are encouraged to conduct when taking on a new role. The New Leader Transition gathers everyone in a room and has the leaders clarify their expectations and explain how they work and how they like to be communicated with. It speeds up by months the process of getting everyone on the same page. Al and I also held a retreat for all the executives, where we did a New Leader Transition with them as well. This is a very effective tool that I wish I had learned about earlier in my career. It just plain speeds up the process of people getting to know you, what you want, how you work, and what is important to you.

In 1995, I created the Disney Great Leader Strategies, and somewhere along the way promoted Dieter Hannig, first to director and then to vice president of food and beverage. Our food and beverage reputation soared after that one decision. I once told Al Weiss that I should get all of the credit for our world-class food and beverage reputation because I put Dieter in the job. He smiled and said, "And I put you in your job!" I'm pretty sure that was a compliment.

Joan Ryan, senior vice president of merchandise, had joined the company just before I came to Orlando. Throughout the years, Joan had reported to virtually everyone, and finally to me as we pulled all operations under one structure. She built a world-class reputation for

Disney in the retail-merchandise business. Joan can tell you a lot about the Big Career Life Roller Coaster, as can Dieter Hannig, Bud Dare, Erin Wallace, Karl Holz, Alice Norsworthy, and Jeff Vahle. Actually, I think if you spoke to every one of my direct reports, you would find that they all had difficult and exciting rides on that Big Career Roller Coaster. I know that Don Robinson, Liz Boice, Rich Taylor, Greg Emmer, Michael Colglazier, and the three people in my office, Chris Bostick, Marsha Davis, and Jeanette Manent, had their own ups and downs on this exciting ride. Today, they are all doing a great job and have their roller coasters under control . . . for the moment anyway.

This is a good lesson in how important it is to get the right people in the right roles. Every one of my direct reports took us from just okay to great during the years we worked together. I was blessed with a world-class team. I never worried about our ability to implement anything, no matter how challenging it may have seemed at the moment. On this count, 9/11 proved me right. Without that team, we could never have accomplished what we did in such a short period of time. Leadership matters!

My team and I learned to appreciate one another and share the leadership position, because it made sense. There are few teams, if any, who can do it the way we did, which is why we achieved spectacular results with every issue that arose and every project we took on. We had total and complete respect for one another as individuals as well as professionals.

In 1996, we received Michael Eisner's approval to spend $6 million to renovate what was then Top of the World restaurant at Disney's Contemporary Resort and to create a brand-new restaurant called the California Grill. That one decision moved us down the path to food and beverage excellence. After that conversion, we had a laboratory to show what we could do. Many other new and exciting concepts followed, enhancing our reputation over the years. Bad food and service are against the law now at the Walt Disney World Resort. Again, exceptional talent made the California Grill exceptional. Without Clifford Pleau, the chef whom I'd hired for the California Grill at the Disneyland Hotel in Paris, and George Miliotes, the restaurant manager, it would have been just another good restaurant. They made it great! The difference between good and great is so big that it cannot be understood until it is experienced.

A few years later, through Joan Ryan's determination, we built a very large World of Disney Store at Downtown Disney. Everyone thought it should be a smaller store except Joan—and she was right. This is one of the greatest stores in the world. Without her persistence, we would have built a much smaller store and would never have realized what we have today.

Don Robinson came back from France after being the general manager of the Newport Bay Club hotel at Euro Disney, where we'd first worked together. Upon his return, he was the opening general manager of Disney's All-Star Resort. He had already been director of rooms for the resorts division. Little did he know or even imagine back then that one day he would be the top executive at the opening of Hong Kong Disneyland. He also could not have known that he would soon be married to Suzy Elrod. Ask Don about the excitement and thrill of the Big Career/Life Roller Coaster. He has had his ups and downs like the rest of us.

You see, everyone has to do it his or her own way. Don had never worked for anyone but Disney for more than thirty years, but he kept up with what was going on in the world and never quit learning. He went on to open the Hong Kong project before leaving Disney for a very successful seven years as president of Baha Mar Resort in the Bahamas, and then, until he retired, as COO of All Aboard Florida, the new high-speed train that will run thirty-two times a day between Miami and Orlando. The business skills Don learned at Disney served him well.

I held the position of senior vice president of operations for the Walt Disney World Resorts from 1993 to 1995. Then Al Weiss was promoted to executive vice president for all of the Walt Disney World Resort, which included all the theme parks and resorts as well as Downtown Disney and the ESPN Wide World of Sports Complex. Not long after that, he was promoted to president. I was promoted to senior vice president of operations for the Walt Disney World Resort; my responsibilities now included the hotels, the theme parks, and all other operating areas. I reported to Bruce Laval, executive vice president of operations for Walt Disney World operations.

We began the process of putting the entire Walt Disney World Resort organization under one structure, reporting up to Al Weiss. This would be the first time that all the businesses were under the responsibility of one person in such an organized way. That would begin the journey to stimulate teamwork and the movement of leaders among all the businesses at the Walt Disney World Resort. It turned out to be the best decision we ever made. It was not accomplished without some pain and some resistance, but it was the right thing to do. *Remember that resistance is not a good reason to stop doing something you believe in. Anytime you're about to do something hard, you can expect resistance.*

I had a lot to learn since I knew nothing about the parks. I knew there were many Disney veterans who wondered why I was even given the job. Slowly but surely, we got the place more and more organized, which meant it was more efficient and more effective. That was the era in which productivity targets were developed. While many people may not like the productivity-target process, I've found it to be one of the most important processes a business can have in place, as long as it is managed in a balanced and flexible way. Every business has to improve its productivity every year, and there's always a better way or a new technology to help make this an attainable target. As long as you balance productivity with employee excellence and guest satisfaction, you will achieve the right business results over the long term.

In May 1997, I was promoted to executive vice president of Walt Disney World operations. Now all support groups and operating groups fell under one organizational structure, and we started to make big progress.

In the ensuing years:

- *We learned how important a clear organizational structure was, as well as the importance of hiring right-fit talent.*

- *We learned the value of using structured interviews before hiring someone, and we worked with the Gallup organization to refine that process. I wish I'd known about structured interviews earlier in my career. We became much more careful about the selection of leaders.*

- *We took on very controversial issues, such as eliminating leads (supervisors) and doing things differently than we had before.*

- *We implemented the Cast Excellence Survey to measure cast satisfaction and give them the leadership, culture, and resources they needed to do their jobs well.*

- *We improved our guest-satisfaction research dramatically.*

We not only taught everyone the importance of being a good leader; we also taught them that we all need to be great. We knew our fellow cast members deserved great leadership so they could deliver world-class service to our guests. The importance of great leadership is the silver bullet for attaining excellent results in any endeavor. I wish I had understood this earlier in my career. We did so much over a few years to improve the Walt Disney World Resort that I sometimes find it hard to believe we accomplished so much so quickly. When you have a great team, you can go faster.

By July 2006, I had been in my current role for almost ten years and had been reporting to Al Weiss for thirteen. I tell people it was almost like being married. He knew me well, and I knew him well. He led me as an individual; he made me feel special, he respected me, and he made me much more knowledgeable. I hope you have a leader like that. It is a lot more fun and much more satisfying.

I was part of a steering committee team that was together for a long time, and we worked well together. We had a real test of teamwork after 9/11, and again after devastating hurricanes hit Orlando in 2004. We went through many challenging times together, but nothing was like 9/11! Al showed what he was made of during that crisis, as did every member of the steering committee. Al took charge and gave us direction while staying cool, calm, and collected. This is exactly what you want in a crisis. It is no time to try to gain consensus. During a crisis, you need one leader, and you need one who acts quickly.

I read recently that during World War II, Winston Churchill set up a separate organization outside the normal bureaucracy that was tasked to do one thing: tell him the truth. Smart man! (This is what chapter 8, Strategy #6 explains in detail in my first book, *Creating Magic*. The title of that chapter is "Learn the Truth.")

We continued to tweak the organizational structure frequently to make sure we were putting right-fit talent in place by following all of the Disney Great Leader Strategies. I learned at the Walt Disney World Resort to pay better attention to the data instead of everyone's personal opinion. Many of the changes we made over the years were fought over and resisted, both internally and externally, because people just hate change. We kept a keen eye on our guest-satisfaction scores as opposed to the noise from people who may have had an unknown agenda or just did not want change to happen. While personal opinion is interesting, it is neither quantitative nor reliable by itself.

We prepared for and went through the infamous Y2K year, holding our breath on December 31, 1999, wondering if the whole world, which had become dependent on computers for everything, would shut down. Nothing at all happened anywhere! Nothing happened even in countries that did not prepare. That day, I watched on television as every time zone in the world celebrated the arrival of the year 2000. I wrote a record of it for my grandchildren as it happened. It was a good, quiet day without incident.

We had troubled times too, as we lost some of our fellow cast members. I remember with sadness that our steering committee had lunch with Frank Wells, president of The Walt Disney Company, on Good Friday, and saw on television two days later, on Easter Sunday, that he had been killed in a helicopter accident. He was a great man.

Over the years, we made great strides in diversity and inclusiveness. We had a long way to go, but we stayed focused on the vital issue of respecting, appreciating, and valuing everyone. This is one of the most important things you can do for your fellow employees, your guests/customers, and your business. My big learning experience here was that I personally had to step up to the responsibility in order to make it happen. By using my position, authority, and communication skills to convince others to get engaged and be proactive, we were able to create the right culture and environment for everyone. I had to take a public position on diversity, as did many other leaders at the Walt Disney World Resort. I hope you have too. You cannot stand in the shadows on this subject if you are in a leadership position.

On July 8, 2006, I had been with Disney for sixteen years. I learned more in those years than I did during the first twenty-five years of my career, and I think I still have many things to learn. By then, I had been working for forty-one years. I had been married for thirty-five years. We had relocated eleven times. We had three grandchildren who lived a mile away. And Priscilla was driving the first new car she'd ever had. We bought it when we moved to Orlando in June, 1993, on the condition that she commit to driving it for ten years. She drove it for thirteen. We loved Orlando. We loved Disney. In fact, Priscilla told me at one point, "Lee, behave yourself and don't get fired, because I like it here."

I calculate that those sixteen years at the Walt Disney World Resort added at least another $5 million to my experience account, which put the total value of my experience at $15 million. The value of experience is safe. It's yours forever. It can't go down in value like the stock market or a house, so it's a worthwhile venture to invest a lot in this area.

In chapter 9, I'll finish this up by explaining why everything that happened to me in my Big Career/Life Roller Coaster ride turned out well . . . *so far!*

Insights

Get the organizational structure right.

Focus on people, training, and culture.

Be the leader you want your children to have when they enter the workforce.

Life After Disney: 2006 Retirement

Wow! That was a fast ride on the Big Career/Life Roller Coaster. The ride started nine chapters ago when I was a twenty-year-old, single, broke college dropout, recently discharged from the United States Army and about to start his first job in the hospitality field as a banquet waiter at the about-to-open Washington Hilton Hotel in Washington, D.C.

Suddenly, it was May 2006, and I was sixty-two years old. I had been married to Priscilla for thirty-eight years; we had a thirty-seven-year-old son, Daniel, a French daughter-in-law, Valerie, and three perfect and adorable grandchildren named Jullian Charles, Margot Sunshine, and Tristan Lee. I particularly like Tristan's middle name. When your children give their children your name, you know you're getting old.

I was in my twenty-fourth professional position. I had worked for three large and famous companies over the previous forty-one years: Hilton Hotels for eight, Marriott International for seventeen, and The Walt Disney Company for sixteen. I was the senior operations executive at Walt Disney World and responsible for all operations. It was a dream job, the job everyone in my industry would love to have, a job I'd never imagined I could attain back in 1965. When I started my career with Hilton, Disney World had not even opened yet.

Our eleven moves included some very interesting and wonderful cities. Priscilla and I enjoyed every place we lived except one, and we were there for only ninety days before I was fired. Our moves, in order, were: Washington, D.C.; Chicago; New York City; Tarrytown, New York; Los Angeles; Lancaster, Pennsylvania; Philadelphia; Chicago; Washington, D.C.; Springfield, Massachusetts; Paris, France; and finally Orlando.

What I did next, at the pinnacle of my career, surprised a lot of people. I left Disney and decided not to pursue positions in other large organizations. I decided there must be more to life than working for big corporations. I was suffering once again from the ailment called boredom. I had been doing the same job for almost ten years.

I decided I wanted to have my own company—no boss, no politics, no cost-management targets, no PowerPoint presentations, no late-night budget meetings, no nothing except what I wanted to do every morning when I climbed out of bed. I decided I wanted to become a writer, public speaker, and teacher. I had been writing for many years and believed that I had a lot of knowledge and experience to share with others, and that I could add great value to their professional and personal lives. Someone once told me there are three ways to leave a legacy: have a baby, write a book, or plant a tree. I still need to plant a tree.

You do not leave a legacy just by attaining some high-level position with a for-profit company unless you are a great teacher and help a lot of people be better and more successful than they ever imagined they could be. The other way is to do something that changes the world, like Steve Jobs or Walt Disney. Your legacy will not be what job you held but what you did for others.

I announced my retirement from Disney to be effective July 28, 2006. Al Weiss organized a wonderful retirement party for me. A lot of my team members and other people stood up and said nice things about me and about my leadership. But the highlight of my retirement was that a window on Main Street USA in the Magic Kingdom was dedicated to me. It's the window right above Uptown Jewelers. I was also given a custom-made, four-foot-high Mickey that had been designed and manufactured in the Central Shops at Disney. It was named Hurricane Mickey because Mickey is wearing a yellow rain slicker and holding a flashlight in one hand and a cell phone in the other. Jeff Vahle, the head of maintenance, and his team picked that Mickey concept to remind me of the many days and nights we spent in the Disney Operational Command Center managing Disney World through the three hurricanes that struck Orlando in 2004.

Before I announced my retirement, I had discussions with the Disney Institute executives and with Al Weiss about becoming an executive speaker for the institute. I also proposed working with the institute for my book about Disney leadership principles. Everyone agreed it would be a good partnership. The Disney Institute created the Executive Speaker Series, of which Marty Sklar, the former head of Disney Imagineering and a fifty-year cast member, and I were members. We were available to speak on behalf of the Disney Institute around the world.

On July 29, 2006, the day after my retirement, I started writing my first book, *Creating Magic: 10 Common Sense Leadership Strategies from a Life at Disney*. I hired a New York literary agent, Lynn Franklin, to represent me with publishers in the US and internationally. I hired a professional writer from California, Phil Goldberg, to write a professional book proposal to submit to publishers and then to take my manuscript and make it a great read. We eventually selected Random House as the US publisher. It took me a little over two years to finish the book. It was released on October 8, 2008.

I hired former Disney cast member John Van Horn to develop a website for me: www.LeeCockerell.com. Jody Maberry manages my *Lessons in Leadership* blog and my podcast, *Creating Disney Magic*, which is on iTunes, Stitcher Radio, and iHeart Radio, in addition to my website. I hired a computer expert, Greg Clayton, to teach me how to be more proficient in using my computer and to take care of any computer problems that come up. I worked with the University of Central Florida to design and print a workbook for my seminars. The workbook is titled *Lessons in Leadership, Management and Customer Service.* I use it to teach day-long and two-day workshops around the world. By the way, I'm different from every other speaker on the circuit in that I do not use PowerPoint. Guess what: my audiences love it. Lesson: *Find ways to stand out and be different from everyone else.*

Creating Magic has sold hundreds of thousands of copies around the world and has been translated into twenty-two languages. Once again, a big and perhaps most important lesson in career magic is to surround yourself with experts who are great at what they do and have the ability to make you great too. I also hired an expert personal trainer, Andrew Noble, to keep me fit. I've been working with him since 2010, twice a week. Today I'm stronger than I was at twenty, and Priscilla has joined me in our workouts. After the age of fifty, strength is more important than aerobics if you don't want to fall and break a hip—and, if you survive the fall, end up in a wheelchair or using a walker for the rest of your life.

In 2012, Random House said they would like me to write another book because *Creating Magic* was doing so well. At first, I wasn't interested in doing that. Writing a book is a lot of work, and I was retired, sort of. But we continued to talk, and I eventually agreed to write my second book on customer service, *The Customer Rules: The 39 Essential Rules for Delivering Sensational Service.* It took Phil Goldberg and me only nine months to finish it. We published *The Customer*

Rules on March 15, 2013. It has been published in fourteen languages so far.

Many public schools, colleges, and universities are using my books in the classroom. We developed a teacher's guide for *Creating Magic* and for *Time Management Magic* for college professors, and we'll soon have a teacher's guide for *The Customer Rules*.

My current work includes public speaking, giving keynote speeches, and day-long seminars to organizations around the world on leadership, management, and customer service.

One of the best things I've been involved in since retiring is volunteering time to work with all branches of our military. I first spoke to twenty army generals fourteen years ago at a leadership conference held by the chief of staff of the US Army at Disney's Yacht Club Resort. Over the years, I have continued to work with them. I even had the privilege of going to Iraq during the war in 2011 to present thirteen workshops on leadership, management, and customer service to troops all over Iraq from north to south, and to State Department employees at the US Embassy in Baghdad. A few years prior to that, I even had the opportunity to do a tandem parachute jump with the Golden Knights army parachute team.

So, as you can see, there is life after dropping out of college, life after the army, life after Hilton, life after being fired, life after being passed over for a big promotion at Marriott, and life after Disney.

Insights

Time flies; get on with it.

Ask yourself: What will my legacy be?

Keep busy in retirement; boredom kills.

As Seen In The Main Street Leader

<u>Courage is the Main Quality of Leadership</u>

"Courage is the main quality of leadership, in my opinion, no matter where it is exercised. Usually, it implies some risk — especially in new undertakings. Courage to initiate something and to keep it going, pioneering and adventurous spirit to blaze new ways, often, in our land of opportunity."

Walt Disney said this a long time ago. He was right on target because courage is a keystone quality of leadership.

One time at Disney, a group of Cast Members came to me to let me know a fellow Cast Member was unhappy because his leader was insensitive and did not follow up on a request he had made.

"Why are you telling me?" I asked. "Why did you not go back to that leader and address the issue? Or, take it to the Human Resources Manager?"

They all looked at me and shook their heads.

"What is it?" I said, wanting to understand.

They explained they were scared to push things too far with their leader because of the possible consequences. I've been there, so I knew what they were talking about. You've probably been there, too. We know it didn't feel good for them to be in that situation.

Here is my challenge to you: Focus on creating an environment where staff feels comfortable pushing back. Make sure you never send a message that something bad will happen to anyone because they speak up and express concerns. Frankly, that is a form of abuse.

Too often, I hear of people being scared to push back.

Here is the truth, though; people do not get fired for speaking up. Not in a company with a reasonable culture. It is an urban legend.

People get fired for poor performance or violating policies around serious issues like drinking, fighting, or theft. Your brain lies to you, don't believe half of what it tells you.

At Disney, I never would have become an Executive Vice President if people were fired for pushing back and saying what they thought. I would have been fired early in my time at Disney. And, the same is true for most of the people who reported to me because they pushed back at me all the time. Trust me, vice presidents at Disney push back hard and often. And frankly, I had the most respect for those who stood up for what they believed in and pushed back when they didn't think I was doing the right thing.

People who pushed back were at the top of the list to get promoted. I needed to know the truth, or I was going to make many bad decisions, and then I really would have been fired. So I would have been crazy not to encourage them to speak the truth and listen to them.

Believe it or not, I am not always right. I wasn't always right at Disney, Marriott, Hilton, or especially at home.

There is a right way and a wrong way to push back. I suggest the professional way, which is to deal with the facts and try to convince your leader why your point of view is important and why they should do what you ask them to do.

At least, you should have your issue heard, have a decision made, and you should be told WHY what you want is not possible – if it turns out that way.

If anyone in your organization feels they will get fired for speaking up, that is the leadership's fault.

Maybe it's your fault.

Put yourself in the place of your direct reports, and ask yourself:

- *"Am I approachable?"*

- *"Do I display a pleasant, calm attitude?"*

- *"Do I ever 'shoot the messenger'?"*

- *"Do I have a reputation for following up and keeping my promises?"*

- *"Do I listen well and understand the issue from the staff's point of view?"*

- *"Am I highly respected and thought of as someone who cares?"*

If you work at an organization that does employee surveys, you can hopefully find the answers to these questions.

Here is a simple test: Would you like the answers you give to your direct reports if you were in the same situation?

The only way we will get better and realize better results is to have a place where everyone is respected, appreciated, valued, made to feel special, treated as an individual, and developed.

Please, I beg of you, work hard on your leadership behaviors.

If you are already a great leader, I'm not talking to you. Well…yes, I'm still talking to you. We can all do more.

If you feel right now that you are not great, and you know you have intimidated employees, then I am definitely talking to you.

Remember, your position and title alone make you, as a leader, somewhat intimidating. Be aware of this. Be careful how you react. Be careful about the look on your face. Thank people for bringing issues to your attention, and most of all, follow-up.

When I was Executive Vice President of Walt Disney World, Cast members would come to see me, and sometimes they would be scared to death just because of my title. I would take the first few minutes to put them at ease by creating a friendly, warm, and focused environment.

With your attitude and actions, you can create an environment and personal reputation that will cause people to have more courage. You, as well as they, will be the winners because of your effort.

Leaders don't have the right to go around making people feel insecure. We are all insecure enough already.

A leader should create an environment to enable staff to deliver good and bad news. This is how trust is formed. Once trust is in place, it will improve performance dramatically. This way, everyone wins.

We all have problems with this, by the way. I remember seeing a cartoon once featuring two lions. Lions are famous for their courage. One lion says to the other, "You make a couple of mistakes in the jungle, and nobody recognizes your scent anymore."

Would your mom be proud of the environment you have set in your jungle?

The Scariest Ride of My Life: 2006–Present

There I was, having the perfect life. I had been retired for two years. I had finished writing my first book. My consulting, teaching, and speaking business was going well. I was healthy and confident about the future—until August 6, 2008, when my whole world started to fall apart.

One Sunday morning a couple of months earlier, Priscilla had told me that her stomach was really hurting and I needed to take her to the emergency room. She had not been feeling well for the previous week or so, and now she was in severe pain. Within ten minutes, we were at the Dr. Phillips Hospital emergency room. By the time we arrived, Priscilla could not even sit in a chair because of the pain. She ended up lying on the floor so she could spread out and eliminate some of the discomfort. The staff did a quick CT scan and found that she had two abscesses on her colon.

She'd had issues with diverticulitis for years, but nothing as serious as that. The doctor admitted her to the hospital.

Over the next two weeks, they pumped her full of powerful antibiotics and finally brought the infections under control so she could be discharged and sent home. Nurses visited for another thirty days to administer more antibiotics. Life slowly returned to normal . . . but not for long.

During the next checkup, the doctor told Priscilla that she needed to have a resection of her sigmoid colon to avoid future recurrences. We scheduled that surgery for August 6, 2008. At eleven o'clock the morning of the operation, I finished recording the audio version of my first book, *Creating Magic*, and went right to the hospital to see Priscilla before she went into surgery. I gave her a kiss, and off she went.

That was the beginning of a two-year nightmare. The surgery went on for three and a half hours. Priscilla stayed in the hospital for five days, and I took her home on August 11. By the morning of the thirteenth, she was in a lot of pain, and to this day she does not remember much about what happened that day.

I called her doctor's office and was told to take her back to the hospital, and they would call to have her admitted.

Here is a time-management story for you. The doctor told me I could take her to the hospital immediately or wait until later that afternoon. I took her right away and got her registered. As it turns out, had I waited until later that afternoon, she would not be here today.

We were registered in the hospital, but there were no rooms available because no patients had been discharged yet. We were taken to a long hallway outside the emergency room, and Priscilla was placed on a gurney. No one came to see her. We were in a "no-man's-land." It was a catch-22: doctors and nurses were everywhere, but no one would treat her because a patient had to be in either the emergency room or a hospital room to be treated.

Leaders Step Up When You Least Expect It

I learned a good lesson about leadership that day, and it was reinforced over the next two years: leaders step up when you least expect it and do the right things no matter how hard it is.

The first leader in this two-year horror story showed up when we needed him most. A doctor who was exiting the emergency room to go on break came toward us. I stopped him and told him Priscilla was being readmitted to the hospital after her resection surgery earlier in the week, but no rooms were available. I explained that no one was treating her and that she was in severe pain and needed pain medication and hydration. He looked at me with concern but said, "I am not supposed to do that."

"Why?"

"You're not in the emergency room."

What he was trying to say, but did not, was that treating a patient in the corridor could cause major legal problems. I told him I understood but that my wife really needed immediate attention. I will never forget what he said: "Okay, I'll do it."

That is what leaders do. They step up and do the right thing instead of worrying about legal issues or anything else, including their own personal safety. As they say, bravery is about being scared and doing it anyway. I suspect that the doctor saved Priscilla's life. He examined her, got her some pain meds, and placed an IV in her.

Priscilla was admitted a couple of hours later. The doctor who examined her told me that, since she was sleeping and her vital signs were perfect, I should just go home. He said they would do a CT scan and assured me that her condition could not be very serious. I went home.

When I returned to the hospital at seven the next morning, Priscilla was not in her room. It took about fifteen minutes for a nurse to find out she was in the intensive care unit. That was the longest fifteen minutes of my life.

It turns out she'd had emergency surgery because the CT scan showed that her first surgery had failed. She woke up seven days later on a ventilator with a colostomy and a wound VAC (vacuum assisted closure), which she would have to wear for the next five months because of an infection caused by the failed bowel resection eight days prior.

I will not tell you all the gory details of what we went through for the next eighteen months. I will tell you that we ran into real leaders over and over again, from incredible nurses and doctors who went far beyond the call of duty, to techs, housekeepers, and cafeteria staff who stepped up time and time again to do more than they were required to do.

Priscilla spent a total of sixty-four days in the hospital. The bill was over $700,000 before adjustments with the insurance company. I have to tell you that one of the greatest blessings was that we still had Cigna health insurance through Disney. Cigna assigned a representative to us, which took a lot of weight off my shoulders. I would give them a score of 10 out of 10. The situation could not have been handled any better. We also had excellent care from the Orlando Regional Medical Center (ORMC) hospital. The nurses, doctors, techs, and support people were all very professional.

Over those eighteen months, I had to take care of Priscilla's every need. She was weak and could not do anything for herself. Plus, we had a colostomy and wound VAC to worry about 24/7. I say "we" because I was intimately involved with these two devices. I also had to get five Ensure protein drinks into Priscilla every day (60 grams of protein total) in order for her to heal, because she had no appetite for normal food. She hated them, but I made her drink them. I also had to get her out of bed three times a day, at 7:00 a.m., noon, and 5:00

p.m., to walk twenty laps through the house with her walker so she would become stronger. She did not want to do that either, but I insisted. We had a few words from time to time.

We all want to crawl back into bed when we don't feel well. I put a new system in place to ensure that she did all twenty laps. I put a table in the hall and called it the tollbooth. I gave Priscilla twenty playing cards and informed her that the toll was one card each time she passed that table. I sat at the toll booth working on my computer and collected the tolls. Only when I got to twenty could she go back to bed. I will not tell you what she said to me when I announced that plan.

Priscilla slowly got better. At one point she was basically back to normal and feeling well. But we still had one big problem. I thought, *She feels great, she looks great, her energy is good, but she still has a colostomy bag hanging on her left side. Now what do we do?* Reversing a colostomy requires major surgery, and it's not always successful. We were scared to death. Then we met another great leader, Dr. Paul Williamson, who was considered by many to be one of the best colorectal surgeons anywhere. We made an appointment to see him. He walked into the room, looked at Priscilla, and said, "Priscilla, you are going to be fine. You are the kind of patient I love to fix."

He had carefully studied her medical file, which by that time was five inches thick. "I consider every one of my patients a gift from God," he said. "No one will touch you in the operating room but me. I will open you, do the surgery, and close you. And I go to the chapel before surgery to get extra help." He went on to say that Priscilla needed another three months of healing time before he could do the surgery.

When that day arrived, Dr. Williamson told us the procedure would take about four and a half hours. It ended up taking *nine* and a half. Every hour, a nurse would come out and keep me updated on how it was going, mainly to reassure me that all was well. When the surgery was completed, Dr. Williamson came out and told me that Priscilla was fine. I asked him why it had taken so long. His answer mirrors what every great leader says when they have done something difficult: "I did what I said I would do. I fixed her, and I gave her a free tummy tuck. I hope she enjoys it. You don't get anything free at Disney."

The final thing I have to tell you about the saga is that I ended up with anxiety and depression and had to be treated for a year and a half with the drug Cymbalta to get back on track. I was lucky to find a great doctor/leader named Roderick Hundley to take care of me. When I first went to see him, I was in pretty bad shape. I was hooked on Ativan, a benzodiazepine for lowering anxiety, as well as sleeping pills. After interviewing me, Dr. Hundley said the sweetest words I had heard in a long time: "Lee, I predict you are going to be fine. You're suffering from situational depression from the long period of stress you've been under with your wife's illness." Those words were similar to what Dr. Williamson had said to Priscilla.

Not only did Dr. Hundley give me encouragement but he also gave me his cell number and home number and told me

I could contact him anytime 24/7 if I was having any issues. Who in the world does that? Leaders do that! He also told me that he was glad that I came in because many men do not seek out help when they need it. He said women do but men resist, and it's a shame because 80 percent of depression can be cured these days. Lesson here, guys: when you need help, go get it.

Summing Up What I've Learned

I think I'll finish by telling you all the things I remember having learned over the years. I hope this will give you food for thought as you ride your Big Career Roller Coaster.

I've learned that in order to have a shot at achieving your goals, you have to take care of your health. In that regard, I've made exercise part of my daily routine, and I schedule it like I do other important appointments. If you're serious, you too will put exercise on your calendar. I've also learned to schedule my annual physical, because no matter how much you exercise, it's important to take preventative measures against disease, and early detection is critical. Annual eye exams and annual dentist checkups need to be scheduled as well. And if you live in a sunny location, like we do in Florida, go see a dermatologist every year too. It's hard to believe that a tiny mole can kill you, but it can.

I'm sure you know it's important to get your teeth cleaned twice a year, and I do that. But I also floss every single day, ever since I read in a dentist's office years ago a sign that said, "Only floss the teeth you want to keep." Flossing saves time, money, and extra visits to the dentist, which is just fine with me. And it only takes about sixty seconds.

Also, for the gentlemen, make sure you get all the tests men hate to get. They're not as bad as the rumors you hear about them, and they're a lot better than the diseases they're meant to detect early. The five big tests for men to have at the appropriate ages are cholesterol (avoid bypass surgeries and heart attacks), colon (avoid cancer), prostate (avoid cancer), blood pressure (avoid strokes and heart attacks), and glucose (avoid diabetes). The survival statistics are not good for men who do not get an annual checkup.

Another thing I've learned is to listen to your doctor and if you trust him or her, do what he or she says: take the right supplements, stop smoking, lose weight, and do anything else that's recommended. If you don't trust your doctor, find another one. At one point, I had been seeing the same doctor for twenty-two years for my annual physical. I could not mislead him because he had my file. I now weigh the same as I did in high school. Staying in tip-top shape may be hard, but when you do the hard things, life gets easier.

Maintaining the correct weight, I think, is even more important than exercise. If you do both, that's even better. Hold on to an old pair of pants and see if you can still get into them ten, twenty, thirty years later. My cholesterol count used to be 230. With exercise, it went down to 173. Now, with the addition of changes in my diet, it's 136. The proof of the pudding is in the tasting. The proof of your health is in the numbers. Do you know your numbers?

I'm writing this to let you know that a large percentage of men do not get an annual physical and often find out too late that something needs attention. Life is short enough already. Why make it even shorter?

Ladies, I'm sorry that I'm not qualified to give you similar advice. Besides, women already do a better job of looking after their health and getting all the right tests. That's why nursing homes have about 180 women and 7 men. Harass those men in your life.

One thing leaders need is high energy, and the key to having more of it is to eat right, exercise every day, and get enough sleep. In warmer areas especially, make sure you drink enough water. When we feel tired, it's often because we're dehydrated, did not get enough sleep, failed to exercise, or just ate a big plate of spaghetti, a loaf of garlic bread, and two pieces of cheesecake. Not getting enough sleep is a thief that steals your energy, your positive attitude, and good decision making. When you don't get enough sleep, you don't feel well, and when you don't feel well, you procrastinate. There might be emotional, mental, or physical impacts. They are all connected, and many sleep-deprived people just get used to the way they feel when they could feel so much better. Read the book *Why We Sleep* and you will learn how to get this part of your life under control. Your energy level will soar, as will the results you are trying to achieve.

I learned another really important thing when I was fifty-eight. For years, Priscilla had told me it's important to stretch and remain flexible. I finally listened to her, and now

I stretch for ten minutes every day. It was hard at first, and no fun. But the results are amazing. So, aerobic exercise, strength training two days a week, and stretching every day—and bingo, I feel a lot better. That's the main reason I expect to be able to work until I'm eighty-five, maybe even longer if I elect to do so and nothing does me in before then. Remember, you have to be alive to make a difference.

What else is important for career magic? One big thing for me has been helping other people. Using your leadership position and authority to help others and making sure you're available when they need you are big deals. Leaders have awesome power over people's lives. A leader can use his or her position and authority to do good things, or bad things, or nothing. Quit being the big, bad boss and become a teacher.

Rosemary Travis at the Gallup organization, while giving me feedback on my Gallup leadership profile years ago, said, "Lee, make sure you always use your talent to do good." That's been a good reminder.

We run into many forks in the road as we travel through life, and leaders, from parents to professional managers, have the ability to help keep others on the right path so they have better lives than they might have had without that direction and assistance. Always remember:

- *Sometimes people just need you to listen.*

- *Sometimes people just need an itty bitty bit of help, such as opening a metaphorical door for them.*

- *Sometimes people need a lot of help that will take much of your time.*

How well leaders (and parents) do these things separates the great ones from the mediocre ones. If you want to leave a worthy legacy behind, make a priority of being available for people when they need you. Help people every chance you get. You may not always be successful, but the least you can do as a leader is try.

I have had eight people in my life thus far who were always there for me when I needed them. Some are family members; some are professional associates. I have made it a point to repay them by being there for other people when I was needed.

What else have I learned so far? One thing is to forget about the chain of command. Most people are not in the military. In working for large organizations, I tried to make it clear to everyone I worked with that I would talk to whomever I want to, and that I expect people to keep me informed directly without worrying about the chain of command. The chain of command can slow things down significantly and deliver less-than-reliable facts and information. The details and emotional content of an issue are not always translated or passed on properly. I'm not saying you should disregard your leader or refuse to give him or her a chance to act when you have a problem. I'm saying that going through the chain of command does not always work.

Leaders who worry about the chain of command structure are usually insecure people who are trying to be in control for some reason. I think it's fine for leaders to say they want to be informed even if it means going outside the chain of command. However, there should never be a hint of intimidation or comments such as "Why did you talk with him without talking with me first?" or "I don't want you telling him anything without checking with me first." The days of working up and down the chain of command are over. Leaders who continue to try to manage this way are doomed to fail or, at a minimum, to be disappointed in their careers. If you suffer from this problem, get over it.

When I was at Walt Disney World, Al Weiss, our direct reports, their direct reports, and I learned to work this way, and we were extremely successful, thanks mainly to this style of managing and leading. My direct reports could talk to Al or whomever they wanted or needed to. As a courtesy, they would leave either Al or me a voice mail with a short summary of the discussion.

Next, do not micromanage. Hire great people. Be clear about their responsibility, authority, and accountability, and then let them do their thing without looking over their shoulders all the time. Micromanaging is a quick way to lose great people!

Shared leadership is a style of leadership whose time has come. Business is simply too complex to play those old command and control games. There are still a lot of leaders out there who don't understand this and actually believe people don't know who they are. This is naive. Everyone knows everything. The last one to figure this out is usually the leader, whom everyone is talking about behind his or her back.

I can tell you that during the crisis of September 11, 2001, and the following weeks, I often let two of my direct reports, Erin Wallace and Karl Holz, take the leadership role if they had the knowledge and expertise required for that moment. I stepped in when it was appropriate and when I could contribute the most. The bottom line is that we did great work using the shared-leadership work style.

Always remember that having the higher salary or fancier title does not make you smarter than your direct reports. I remember Ken Blanchard, the leadership and management author, wearing a button that read, "None of us is as smart as all of us."

This brings me to another thing I've learned about career development—something that's a strength of mine. It's called "self-awareness." I don't know if this can be learned or not, but individuals who don't have it are doomed. If they have behavioral or personality traits that are seen as negative and fail to figure that out, they suffer from a lack of self-awareness and, unfortunately, keep doing the same things over and over.

That's why it's so important for leaders to give people feedback on their performance, including their personality and behavioral traits. Some will never figure it out unless they receive frequent, candid feedback. In this area, we all have plenty of work to do.

Many people lack self-awareness because they're simply not getting feedback; others lack self-awareness because they don't listen to the feedback they get. I know for sure that what may be considered a minor personality or behavioral trait has ruined many a career, and often the person never even knows why. Help your leader or partner give you feedback by asking for it and then accepting it in a gracious way, without getting defensive. It may be the best thing that ever happens to you.

Can anyone understand how some leaders continue to try to lead in a way that's in direct conflict with the behaviors we wanted to instill at the Walt Disney World Resort? To me, this is on a par with drinking and driving, texting and driving, or not wearing your seat belt. It's dangerous!

Another thing I've learned about career development is to try to do a big, hard thing from time to time. Take on projects that will make a big difference. For example, here are some of things I've done: develop the Disney Great Leader Strategies; teach time-management courses to all cast members; start the Cast Excellence lunches as a forum for learning; create the Main Street Diary; and make major changes to the organizational structure.

A lesson that's a close cousin to that one is to pick no more than three things that interest you and become known for them. Three things I've developed expertise in, outside of my normal duties, are: time management, leadership, and service management. I have a thriving business today based on my expertise in those three areas.

No matter what field or area I might want to spend time in, these three skills offer great value to me as a leader. People actually think I'm an expert in those areas, and you know what? I *am* an expert because I've spent years and years reading, studying, going to classes, teaching, and practicing. If you focus on something for long enough, you can become a known expert in it. I've also focused on learning to be an effective communicator through storytelling, and I hope you agree that I've achieved some level of success in that endeavor.

I did not begin to focus on these things until 1980, when I was thirty-six years old, so it's never too late. Colonel Sanders did not start Kentucky Fried Chicken until he was retired and sixty-nine. The world is full of examples of late starters who made a huge difference in their area of focus. You can do this too, in small or large ways, if you think about it and focus on it. It will broaden your future opportunities as well.

Remember, the more you know, the more you're worth. That's the reason many say, "Knowledge is power." I might also add that "Shared knowledge is even more powerful."

Share the things you know with others. This is called teaching.

There are too many people in business who think that keeping knowledge to themselves is power. You can see what happened when the FBI and CIA did not share information with each other about the knowledge they had surrounding terrorist movements that may have led to the events of 9/11. I assure you there was not an environment in place where people felt free to speak up until a woman had the courage to write a letter to the FBI director about the lack of follow-through on things her office and her supervisors knew. She showed real leadership and courage by stepping up and doing the right thing. I think I'll send copies of the Disney Great Leader Strategies to the heads of the homeland security agencies. What do you think?

Another thing I've learned is to be flexible and not try to win every battle. There's a time to let things go and see how they work out. Save some of your bullets for the big battles. Don't fall on your sword for every issue. Most things can be reversed later if they don't work out. Nobody likes to work with someone who always has to win no matter what. Don't just use your position to win; use it to teach and influence others for good. A good way to practice this is to play hide-and-go-seek or other games with children, and let them win—not all of the time but most of the time—until they're old enough to be competitive.

Another thing I learned later in my career is to block out time on your calendar to think. Go to the library or some other quiet place for a minimum of four hours and just think about what you should be focusing on in your life. This is called "time to muse."

Final Fun and Serious Insights

Have friends of all ages, backgrounds, religions, and cultures.

Help your family and friends as much as you can.

Be gentle with children. A child spilling milk is not a federal offense—that's why they invented paper towels.

Spilling a glass of red wine on a white carpet *is* a federal offense. Your spouse will not forgive you.

Make your boss look good.

Give credit where credit is due. Practice appreciation, recognition, and encouragement (A.R.E.).

Do not take yourself too seriously (humor is a good thing).

Do not fall in love with your title unless it's grandfather or grandmother (or something equivalent; you know what I mean).

Don't get personal. Keep it professional.

Take on tough assignments. You have more to gain from them in the long run.

Call or write your parents often (or text them in this day and age).

Bring solutions to your leader, not just problems.

Brag about your children and grandchildren, and make people look at pictures of them.

Use your authority to do good things.

Listen more and talk less.

Experience things just to experience them.

Do not do anything while driving other than drive (don't text, drink, or put on makeup).

Give gifts to your grandchildren on *your* birthday. Do not underestimate the influence you have on them.

Know when you shift from persistent to annoying.

Don't tell edgy jokes or say something hurtful and then say, "I was kidding." By then it's too late.

Be candid, but do it with finesse.

Do not let your kids watch television or play on their computers or phones if they have school the next day. They'll turn out to be better readers, which converts to better students and better adults.

Remember that much of what you believe is not true. Take a hard look at your deepest beliefs.

Do not hurt people's feelings.

Do not push your direct reports around. They will get you fired.

Play games with children, and watch cartoons with them.

Never say *never*.

Use the word *no* sparingly.

Seek the truth! All stories sound right in isolation.

Tell the people you appreciate that you appreciate them . . . often.

Tell the people you love that you love them . . . often.

Find creative ways to let people know how much you appreciate them, including your leaders, your spouse or partner, and children.

Laugh, cry, and smile a lot.

Put IOUs in those plastic Easter eggs for your children or grand-children, such as a visit to the bookstore, a pancake breakfast, or a trip to the Apple Store.

Give your grandchildren candy after they eat their breakfast, even if it's 6:30 a.m.. But make sure their parents are still asleep.

Do not blame others for the predicaments you get yourself into.

Wear little pointed paper hats at family birthday parties, and always have balloons.

Know what you're good at, and do those things most of the time.

Do not use your position to try to intimidate people. Your position is intimidating enough already.

Do not give up too soon.

Wear your seat belt.

Do hard things. If you do, life will become easier. If you do only easy things, life will get harder.

Remember, it's never too late to get better.

That's enough for now! I told you I would tell you how everything has come together in my career and how I now think about all those ups and downs and aches and pains I've had to deal with over the years. I want you to know that each of them was important in getting me to where I am today:

If I had not dropped out of college, I would not have gone into the army at Fort Poke, Louisiana.

And finally, "Do your best and forgive yourself."

If I had not gone into the army, I would not have met Terrance Biggs in cook's school; he recommended that I go to Washington, D.C., with him to get a job at the Washington Hilton. I also would not have met Graham Cromack. We later became roommates in Washington, D.C., before he returned to the UK. I recently reconnected with him through Google and found out he was living in Spain.

If I had not gone to the Washington Hilton, I would not have started to gain the experiences that taught me so much over the years and prepared me for every promotion I received. That first job was like the foundation of a building. Each experience after that built upon the previous. I'm now a twenty-four-story building, so to speak . . . or maybe even taller.

If I had not gone to the Washington Hilton, I would not have met Priscilla, and we would not have fallen in love and gotten married. Also, if I had not been persistent, we would not be married now either.

If we had not gotten married, we would not have our son,
Daniel.

If I had not accepted that low-paying clerk's job in the food
control office in Washington, giving up a lucrative job as a banquet server, I would not have become a manager and gotten
promoted to Chicago, where Daniel was born.

If I had not gone to Chicago, I would not have had enough
experience to be promoted to the Waldorf Astoria.

If I had not gone to New York, I would not have had a leader
like Gene Scanlan, who took me under his wing, mentored me,
and promoted me to assistant director of food and beverage at
the most famous hotel in the world.

If I had not done good work at the Waldorf, I would not have
been promoted to executive assistant manager and director of
food and beverage of the Tarrytown Hilton.

If I had not gone to Tarrytown and had a relationship problem
with my boss, I would not have ended up at the Los Angeles
Hilton as director of food and beverage.

If I had not had another leader whom I did not respect or learn
anything from, I would not have quit and gone to that hotel
in Lancaster, Pennsylvania, where I got fired ninety days later
and learned a good life lesson.

If I had not been fired in Lancaster, I would not have ended up
with a great seventeen-year career at Marriott.

If I had not had some political relationship problems late in my career at Marriott and been passed over for a promotion, I would not have ended up in Springfield, Massachusetts, as a hotel general manager.

If I had not done a great job in Springfield, I would not have been offered the job with Disney as director of food and beverage in Paris.

If I had not gone to Paris, my son would not have come to France after graduating from college, which means he would not have met Valerie.

If Daniel had not met Valerie, I would have missed out on the biggest and most important promotion of my life: to the position of grandfather in 1995, 1998, and 2001.

If all those things had not happened to me in the exact order they did, I would not have ended up at the Walt Disney World Resort in the best role I ever had—except for husband, father, father-in-law, and grandfather, of course.

And finally, if I hadn't gone to Disney, I would not have gained the experience and credibility to write four books and start my own company.

This is the first time in my life that I'm totally satisfied with what I'm doing. I am very lucky. I consider myself blessed to be working with so many professionals around the world. Someone recently asked me to describe my life in one word. That word is *complete*!

It took a while to get here, and I had to overcome many obstacles and barriers, but I did it my way. You need to do the same. Best advice ever: *"Do it your way—and don't ever give up!"*

See the graph on the next page that shows what the Big Career/ Life Roller Coaster looked like for me. This ride has been going for more than seventy-eight years so far. As you can see, there have been many thrilling and scary rides since the ride first launched! Good luck to you as you take your own rides.

Insights

Life is unpredictable.

You can control much of your life.

You are not a product of your circumstances; you are a product of your decisions.

LEE COCKERELL RESOURCES

Great leaders look for the better way, every day!

Go to www.LeeCockerell.com for additional resources on leadership, management and service excellence, including my Lessons in Leadership blog, my Creating Disney Magic podcast, my Cockerell Academy online learning system, my monthly newsletter, *The Main Street Leader,* and my books, *Creating Magic: 10 Common Sense Leadership Strategies from a Life at Disney; The Customer Rules: The 39 Essential Rules for Delivering Sensational Service; Time Management Magic: How to Get More Done Every Day and Move from Surviving to Thriving;* and *Hardwiring Magic.*

There is a wealth of information available to assist you in strengthening your leadership skills. Study and read about leadership and management every day. The more you put in your mind about these subjects, the more resources you will be able to call on when you're faced with difficult issues in your life. You have to know more to be more and do more.

★ ★ ★

Please contact Lee Cockerell at Lee@LeeCockerell.com for keynote addresses, workshops, consulting, executive coaching, and seminars on leadership, management, culture, and world-class customer service. Phone: 407-908-2118.

Lee's Career and Life Roller Coaster

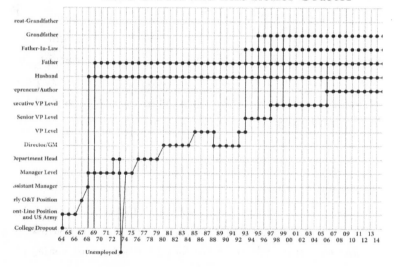

About the Author

Lee Cockerell is the former executive vice president of operations for the Walt Disney World Resort. As the senior operating executive for ten years, Lee led a team of forty thousand cast members and was responsible for the operations of twenty resort hotels, four theme parks, two water parks, a shopping and entertainment village, and the ESPN sports  and recreation complex, in addition to the ancillary operations that supported the number one vacation destination in the world.

One of Lee's major and lasting legacies was the creation of Disney Great Leader Strategies, which was used to train and develop the seven thousand leaders at Walt Disney World. Prior to joining Disney in 1990 to open the Disneyland Paris project, Lee held various executive positions in the hospitality and entertainment business, at Hilton Hotels & Resorts for eight years and Marriott International for seventeen years. He served for eight years in the United States Army Reserves.

Lee has served as chairman of the board of heart of Florida United Way, as a member the board of trustees for the Culinary Institute of America (CIA), and as a board member of the Production and Operations Management Society and Reptilia, a Canadian attractions-and-entertainment company. He has also served on the board of advisors for the business school at Oklahoma State University and at Rollins College. In 2005, Governor Jeb Bush appointed Lee to the Governor's Commission on Volunteerism and Public Service for the State of Florida, where he served as chairman of the board.

He now dedicates his time to public speaking and authoring books on leadership, management, and service excellence. His first book, *Creating Magic: 10 Common Sense Leadership Strategies from a Life at Disney*, is now available in twenty-two languages. He also wrote *The Customer Rules: The 39 Essential Rules for Delivering Sensational Service*.

Lee performs leadership and service-excellence workshops and offers consulting services for organizations around the world as well as for the Disney Institute.

Lee has received the following awards:

★ *Golden Chain Award for Outstanding Leadership and Business Performance from the Multi-Unit Foodservice Operations Association (MUFSO)*

★ *Silver Plate Award for Outstanding Operator in the foodservice industry from the International Foodservice Manufacturers Association*

★ *The Martin K. Starr Excellence in Production and Operations Management Practice Award from the Productions and Operations Management Society (POMS)*

★ *Grandfather of the year from his three grandchildren, Jullian, Margot, and Tristan*

Please contact Lee Cockerell at Lee@LeeCockerell. com for keynote addresses, workshops, consulting, executive coaching, and seminars on leadership, management, and world-class customer service. Phone: 407-908-2118.

COCKERELL
ACADEMY

This book comes with the first edition of The Main Street Leader for FREE:

Scan the QR code below or download at:
www.leecockerell.com/msl

(Open your phone's camera and place it over this image as if you are about to take a photo. Your camera will scan it and prompt you to open our website)

This edition of The Main Street Leader features articles on purpose vs. role, keeping your promises as a leader, and more. Plus, my favorite article; Advice From Mother.

Other Resources by Lee Cockerell

Creating Magic

*10 Common Sense Leadership Strategies From
A Life At Disney - Based on the principles taught
at the World Renowned Disney Institute.*

Creating Magic shows all of us – from small business owners to managers at every level – how to inspire employees, delight customers and achieve extraordinary business results just like Lee did at *Disney World*.

Creating Magic by Lee Cockerell – 270 pages
Available in Hardback, Paperback, E-book and Audio Book

The Customer Rules

*The 39 Essential Rules for Delivering
Sensational Service*

Lee shares indispensable rules for serving customers with consistency, efficiency, creativity, sincerity and distinction. Lee shows why the customer always rules and presents instructions for serving customers so well they'll never want to do business with anyone but YOU.

The Customer Rules by Lee Cockerell – 208 pages
Available in Hardback, Paperback, E-book and Audio Book

Time Management Magic

How to Get More Done Every Day and Move from Surviving to Thriving

The executive time-management secrets in this book will help you keep all parts of your life under control and jump-start your personal and professional growth. It is not just about time management. It is about life management.

Time Management Magic by Lee Cockerell - 144 pages
Available in Hardcover, Paperback, and e-book.

Hardwiring Magic

How to Stay on Track to Achieve a Stellar Career

A unique book full of priceless advice and insightful experience. Lee Cockerell chronicles how he went from being a college dropout, rose through the ranks at both *Hilton* and *Marriott*, and ultimately became the Executive Vice President of Operations for *Walt Disney World*® Resorts.

Hardwiring Magic, co-author – 66pages
Available in Paperback and E-book

Available at www.LeeCockerell.com, Online Retailers and Bookstores Nationwide

CPSIA information can be obtained
at www.ICGtesting.com
Printed in the USA
JSHW021326210822
29567JS00002B/25